EVERYDAY LIFE

IN

19TH-CENTURY

IRELAND

EVERYDAY LIFE
IN
19TH-CENTURY
IRELAND

IAN MAXWELL

The
History
Press
Ireland

First published 2012

The History Press Ireland
50 City Quay
Dublin 2
Ireland
www.thehistorypress.ie

British Library Cataloguing in Publication Data.
A catalogue record for this book is available from the British Library.

ISBN 978 1 84588 743 8

Typesetting and origination by The History Press

CONTENTS

INTRODUCTION

By the beginning of the nineteenth century, Britain had held a strong presence in Ireland for more than seven centuries, and yet that impoverished
near neighbour remained to most Englishmen a remote, if not sinister, place.
English barrister George Cooper, writing in 1799 declared, 'remote corners
of the Hebrides have been often explored … [and] the name of Ireland is
most familiar to our ears, yet both the kingdom and its inhabitants have been
as little described as if the Atlantic had flowed between us.' Almost twenty

Dublin Bay.

years later, John Curwen MP remarked that he was visiting a country that, 'although almost within our view, and daily in our contemplation, is as little known to me, comparatively speaking, as if it were an island in the remotest part of the globe.' Most Englishmen preferred to stay at home where their contact with the Irish was confined to those they encountered in the streets of London or in many of the growing industrial towns of the Midlands, the North of England and the central lowlands of Scotland. They associated them with poverty, crime, drunkenness and Catholicism which helped create the stereotype of the stage Irishman.

Nineteenth-century accounts of Ireland conjured up images as alien to their readers in the drawing rooms of London, Manchester and Birmingham as the deserts of Western Australia or the hinterland of Africa. American missionary Asenath Nicholson admitted as much when she came to Ireland on the eve of the Great Famine; 'When we reached Dublin Bay, I gave myself to rummaging the scanty knowledge I had of Ireland, to ascertain whether I knew anything of its true condition and character.' She went on breathlessly:

> I knew that between the parallels of 51 and 55 of north latitude there is a little green spot, in the ocean, defended from its surging waves by bold defying rocks; that over this spot are sprinkled mountains, where sparkle the diamond and where sleep the precious stone; glens, with rich foliage and pleasant flowers, where the morning song of the bird is blending with the playful rill; that through its valleys and hillsides were embedded the gladdening fuel and the rich mine; that over its lawns and wooded parks were skipping the light-footed fawn and bounding deer; that in its fat pastures were grazing the proud steed and the noble ox; that on its healthy mountain slopes the nimble goat and the more timid sheep find their food. I knew that proud castles and monasteries, palaces and towers, tell the passer-by that here kings and chieftains struggled for dominion, and priests and prelates contended for religion; and that the towering steeple, and the more lowly cross, still say that the instinct of worship yet lives, that here the incense of prayer and the song of praise continue to go up.

She did admit, 'I had been told that over this fair landscape hangs a dark curtain of desolation and death; that the harp of Erin lies untouched, save by the finger of sorrow, to tell what music was once in her strings; that the tear is on her cheek she sits desolate, and no good Samaritan passes that way, to pour in the oil and wine of consolation.' She was soon to encounter poverty on a scale she had never imagined.

To those visitors who braved the unknown, nineteenth-century Ireland was a world of extremes. The Irish countryside was made up of great estates where, by the 1870s, more than half the land was owned by fewer than 1,000 major landlords, many of them related to each other blood or marriage. Served by an army of servants, they enjoyed a luxurious and leisurely lifestyle, housed in mansions with richly furnished interiors and elaborate gardens. For the vast majority, however, life was one of grinding poverty. By 1841, 40 per cent of the houses in Ireland were one-room mud cabins. Furniture in these mud cabins usually consisted of a bed of straw, a crude table and stool and a few cooking utensils. The largest group found in the countryside and at the bottom of the social scale were the agricultural labourers, many of whom were casually employed and who tramped the roads in search of work during the 'hungry months'.

It was a world which, at the beginning of the nineteenth century, seemed for ever set in stone, as conjured up in the words of Dublin hymn writer Cecil Alexander in *All Things Bright and Beautiful*:

> The rich man in his castle,
> The poor man at his gate,
> God made them high and lowly,
> And ordered their estate.

Navvies, County Donegal. (Samuel G. Bayne *On An Irish Jaunting-Car Through and Connemara*, 1902)

It turned out to be a less than prophetic view. The nineteenth century would usher in a period of monumental change in Ireland. The railways which were laid out through the famine-stricken countryside would transform the local economy, providing employment, developing towns and giving the impetus for Ireland's first tourist boom. An amazed traveller towards the end of the century would declare:

> To any part of the island the railways convey us with as much comfort as on the best English lines. At the remotest towns and villages the post arrives with laudable regularity, and the electric-telegraph wires reach to every corner where there are English-speaking inhabitants. At the railway stations there are bookstalls, with newspapers and miscellaneous literature; and the travel-ler, whether commercial or non-commercial, will notice no great differences from what he has been accustomed to in provincial journeys in England. In some things, and these not unimportant – such as police, primary schools, workhouse buildings and management – he will even be forced to admit superiority in Ireland. If he asks no questions about church and chapel, and reads no local newspapers, he would hardly feel that he was in a strange country, and cannot realize all he has heard about Irish wrongs and Irish wretchedness, and about the hopeless difficulty of governing a country apparently so civilised and prosperous.

There were many at the time that would have disputed such a rosy account of Ireland in the 1870s. Only a few years before, both Irish and English newspa-pers had been awash with rumours of illegal arms shipments and impending rebellion. In the countryside, agrarian violence was commonplace in many parts of the country as landlords evicted their tenants in increasing numbers. In an attempt to address these grievances, British governments would issue a series of land laws which, by the beginning of the twentieth century, would lead to the end of the great estates in favour of small, family-owned farms.

A succession of British governments also took an increasingly interven-tionist role in education and social reform. A National School system was established across the country which provided free elementary education for all children, a full four decades before the establishment of a similar system in England. For those less fortunate, the Irish Poor Law system would help eradicate the perennial problem of begging and vagrancy by incarcerating entire families behind the forbidding walls of the workhouses which were established in every market town.

Within a generation life in Ireland had changed irrevocably for many. By the end of that eventful century the hated tithe proctor had long vanished;

the hedge school, the swarms of beggars, public hangings, faction fighting and the sound of the banshee had all but vanished from the landscape. Looking back over the century, James Macauley observed in his book *Ireland in 1872* that Ireland had changed beyond all recognition from the Ireland popularised by writers such as Charles Lever and William Charleton, which enjoyed great success with English audiences: 'The rollicking, reckless, fighting, fox-hunting squire or squireen; the half-pay captain of dragoons, professional duelist, gambler, and scamp; the punch-imbibing and humorous story-telling priest; the cringing tenantry and lawless peasantry; how unreal and unrepresentative all these characters seem now!'

On the other hand, some things did not change. Religious rivalries between the communities would become an increasing problem from the late eighteenth century. By the nineteenth century faction fighting at local fairs had spread to major centres like Belfast where sectarian violence would reflect the increasingly polarised nature of politics throughout Ireland. 'In this unhappy country', wrote James Johnson in *A Tour in Ireland* (1844), 'RELIGION, instead of cementing Christians together in one common faith and friendship, appears to be a corrosive agent that dissolves all cementing ties, and repulses man from man.' Even those like William Le Fanu who considered the nineteenth century to be one of unimpeded progress conceded, 'Since my early days I have seen a vast improvement in everything but intolerance in religion; that, I grieve to say, is as strong as ever.'

Although by the end of the nineteenth century Ireland had become a less remote place, to those who administrated the country it remained a puzzle. James Macauley summed up the Irish conundrum very succinctly:

> Ireland is peaceful: yet nearly a fifth of the British army has to be quartered there, as in a hostile country.
>
> Ireland is loyal: yet it sometimes returns as members of Parliament disloyal traitors and even convicted felons, as a defiance and insult to the English nation …
> Ireland is prosperous: yet it remains the difficulty and the despair of British statesmen.
>
> How are these paradoxes to be explained?

This book aims to examine those paradoxes and, although the past cannot always be easily explained even in retrospect, to make clear that Ireland in the nineteenth century was no less complex, beguiling, intriguing and exasperating than it is today.

1

THE UNION

At the beginning of the nineteenth century the Irish Parliament was fighting for its survival. It had a long but not particularly distinguished history. The earliest known Irish Parliament for which there is a definitive record met on 18 June 1264 at Castledermot in County Kildare. For the next 500 years it carried out its business to the complete indifference of the vast majority of the country's inhabitants. But it did so in some style. It sat in the world's first purpose-built two-chamber Parliament House, opened in 1737, while their counterparts in London were forced to make do with the cramped conditions and odd seating arrangements of the ancient Palace of Westminster.

Membership of the House was as exclusive as Dublin society. It was for the privileged, rich and strongly Anglican. Sessions of Parliament drew many of the wealthiest of Ireland's Anglo-Irish ascendancy to Dublin, particularly as sessions often coincided with the Irish social season, running from January to 17 March, when the Lord Lieutenant presided over state balls in Dublin Castle. Leading peers in particular flocked to Dublin, where they lived in enormous and richly decorated town houses, initially on the north side of Dublin, later in new Georgian residences around Merrion Square and Fitzwilliam Square. Their presence in Dublin, along with large numbers of servants, provided a regular boost to the city's economy

The Irish Parliament was not truly independent because the executive branch of government, the Lord Lieutenant, was appointed by the Crown and was not answerable to the Parliament. Poyning's Law, imposed on Ireland in 1495, restricted the Irish Parliament from taking action on any law that was not pre-certified by the Crown. It was only during the last twenty years of its existence that the Irish Parliament, led by MP Henry Grattan, persuaded the Crown to allow it more independence. The Irish Constitution of 1782 modi-fied Poyning's Law, allowing the Irish Parliament virtual Home Rule authority.

This independence was short lived. The United Irish Society, or United Irishmen, founded at Belfast in 1791 by Theobald Wolfe Tone, was formed by those who demanded parliamentary reform and the removal of English control over Irish affairs. The organisation at first aimed at legislative reform but, after the society was suppressed in 1794, it became a secret revolutionary organisation. The British government waged a campaign of brutal repression in Ulster in an attempt, largely successful, to break up the cohesive centre of the movement. In March 1798 several southern leaders were arrested, and when rebellion did break out in May it was in isolated sporadic bursts. The only appreciable success was in County Wexford, but the rebels there were defeated in the battle of Vinegar Hill on 21 June. The Rising had already collapsed in the south and west of Ireland, when the standard was raised in the north. In County Antrim an army of some 3,000 and 4,000 men under Henry Joy McCracken was crushed, but in County Down the rebels succeeded in occupying Saintfield. They were soon dislodged, however, by government forces under the command of Major-General George Nugent. Having burned Saintfield to the ground, Nugent's troops reached Ballynahinch on the following day and proceeded to bombard the town. On the morning of 13 June 1798 the rebels' ammunition ran out and Nugent's army overwhelmed them on Ednavady Hill. No mercy was shown and Nugent later claimed to have killed 300 in the fighting and a further 200 in the pursuit. With the town a smoking ruin and bodies lying unburied in the streets, the rising in County Down was over.

What particularly concerned the British government was the fact that during this period Republican France had attempted three invasions of Ireland, once in 1796 under General Hoche, and twice in 1798 under General Humbert and Admiral Bompart. This posed a very serious security threat, not only to Britain but to the Empire as well, which the government could not ignore. Prime Minister William Pitt lost no time after the 1798 Rebellion in bringing forward his scheme for a union between the British and Irish parliaments. There were impassioned debates in the Irish Parliament but these were concerns of the Irish Establishment, mostly the nobility, the gentry and office holders. Lord Lieutenant Viscount Cornwallis was near the mark when he said, 'The mass of the people of Ireland do not care one farthing about the Union.'

Support for the Union came from two very different constituencies. One of these – the Protestant – after the fright it received in 1798, saw the Union as a greater safeguard of their interests. Ironically, many Catholic landowners and middle-class Catholics favoured the Union on the grounds that they would be better accommodated by a more tolerant Protestant majority in England than by an insecure Anglo-Irish minority in Ireland. Prime Minister

Louth Castle, Bellingham.

William Pitt fully intended to follow the Act of Union with other reforms including Catholic Emancipation which would address their aspirations. It was for this reason that, although the grand lodge of the Orange Order in Dublin attempted to remain neutral on the Union, thirty-six lodges from Armagh and Louth alone petitioned against it. It mattered very little. On 28 March 1800 the terms of the Union were agreed by both houses of the Irish Parliament and the Act of Union came into force on 1 January 1801. A new country was formed (The United Kingdom of Great Britain and Ireland) with a new flag, the Union Jack, created from the flags of each member state. In time, Protestants came to accept that their best hopes of preserving their position in Ireland lay in the preservation of the Union, while this fact alone convinced Catholics that the repeal of the Union offered their best opportunity for advancing their interests.

At the same time, the passing of the Union turned out to be something of an anti-climax. From all over the country, including Dublin, reports came of perfect tranquillity. There was, however, one last attempt to revive the cause of the United Irishmen, a remnant of which remained opposed to the British connection whether there was a Union are not. The rising of July 1803 was led by Robert Emmet who had hoped to assemble 2,000 men to attack Dublin Castle. In the end, he could only muster eighty, most of whom, one later admitted, had been in the Yellow Bottle tavern, 'drinking and smoking, in the highest spirits, cracking jokes, and bantering one another, as if the business they were about to enter on was a party of pleasure.'

'Real Thing'. (Samuel G. Bayne, *On An Irish Jaunting-Car Through Donegal and Connemarra*, 1902)

The rising in Dublin turned out to be little more than a street riot. Emmet, appalled by the brutishness into which his bid to establish an Irish Republic immediately degenerated, abandoned the project and took himself off into hiding where he remained for a month before being caught, tried and executed. His speech from the dock, which immortalised him in Irish history, included a phrase which would reverberate down through Irish history, 'Let no man write my epitaph … When my country takes her place among the nations of the earth, then and not till then let my epitaph be written.'

The 1798 Rebellion and Emmet's failed rising remained fresh in many minds, and not only those of the authorities, for many years afterwards. John Gamble, who travelled through Ireland in 1812, found that old animosities remained. While staying at Banbridge, County Down, he got into conversation with a local man at the market house. As they talked:

> a party of yeomen, drums beating, and colours flying, passed us. They splashed through the wet to quick time, and looked as jaded and dirty as a company in a ball room, when day breaks on them. Though their looks were impaired, their loyalty was not. At sight of us their music changed to 'Croppies lie down' my new acquaintance smiled I asked him the reason. He was, it seems, suspected of being a united Irishman in the year 1798, and these loyal gentlemen took this method, he supposed, of rebuking him for his past transgressions. I drank tea with him, and found him an intelligent man, perfectly awakened from the reveries of republicanism, if he had ever indulged in them, though he complained heartily of the pressure of the times, and the exactions of landlords.

It was County Kerry barrister Daniel O'Connell, who had developed an early reputation for radical politics, who would resurrect the anti-Union cause out of the ashes of the 1798 and Emmet Risings. He was determined to use the machinery of Parliament to obtain political and religious equality. In the space of just over twenty years he inaugurated two great political campaigns in succession. The first was for Catholic Emancipation, or the removal of the remnants of legal discrimination against Catholics surviving from the Penal Laws. Principally, this concerned the right of Roman Catholics to sit in parliament, from which they were still banned unless they took an oath abjuring certain fundamental Catholic beliefs. The second, more daunting objective, was the repeal of the Act of Union itself.

To campaign for Catholic Emancipation, O'Connell built up a strong mass organisation with the help of able middle-class assistants and, more importantly still, the Roman Catholic clergy. He set up many organisations to raise money for the cause of Emancipation, including the Catholic Association in 1823. An essential feature of O'Connell's political organisation was its broad democratic basis. Associate membership of the Association could be had for a penny a month and soon very large sums were flowing into it. Although 1798 had left him with a horror of popular violence, he stressed at mass rallies the physical power he had under his control. In June 1843 he announced the following to more than 300,000 supporters at Kilkenny:

Robert Emmet.

> I stand today at the head of a group of men sufficient, if they underwent military training, to conquer Europe! Wellington never had such an army. [Cheers] There was not at Waterloo on both sides as many brave and determined men as I see before me today. Tell them what to do and you have them disciplined in an hour. [Cheers.] They are as well able to walk in order after a band as if they wore red coats.

In 1828, O'Connell was elected to represent County Clare, causing wild popular excitement. However, because he was Catholic, he could not take his seat without taking the Oath of Supremacy which recognised the King as head of the Church. This was something that O'Connell as a devout Catholic would not do. The British Government, fearing a civil war or serious disorder in Ireland because of intense opposition to the existing anti-Catholic legislation, passed the Roman Catholic Relief Act (1829) which granted Catholic Emancipation. The legislation was not retrospective, forcing O'Connell to stand again, this time in County Kerry where he was elected unopposed.

O'Connell initially concentrated on building up an effective Parliamentary organisation. In return for his support, and that of thirty-nine of the Irish MPs returned in the General Election of 1832, he agreed to support Lord Melbourne and his Whig Government in return for significant Irish reforms. Although the Whigs passed a Tithe Commutation Act (1838) and the Irish Municipal

Reform Act (1840), O'Connell thought this inadequate. He was also totally opposed to the passing of the Irish Poor Law Act and when the Whigs refused to change it, he withdrew his support for the Government. O'Connell turned instead to the mass following he had retained in Ireland. He announced that 1843 would be the Year of Repeal. The Catholic Church rallied to the cause, led by Archbishop MacHale of Tuam. The most notable characteristic of the repeal movement was the massive outdoor meeting attended by hundreds of thousands of supporters. The first of these was held at Trim in March 1843 where he told an enthusiastic crowd:

> I admit there is the force of a law, because it has been supported by the policeman's truncheon, by the soldier's bayonet, and by the horseman's sword; because it is supported by the courts of law and those who have power to adjudicate in them; but I say solemnly, it is not supported by constitutional right. The Union, therefore, in my thorough conviction, is totally void, and I avail myself of this opportunity to announce to several hundreds of thousands of my fellow subjects that the Union is an unconstitutional law and that it is not fated to last long – its hour is approaching.

King O'Connel at Tara. (*Punch*, 26 August 1843)

Daniel O'Connell standing trial in 1844.

The Government was alarmed but Prime Minister Robert Peel was not so easily intimidated. In May 1843, he told the House of Commons that he was authorised by the Queen to say that, '… deprecating as I do all war, and especially civil war, there is no alternative which I do not think preferable to the dismemberment of the Empire'. O'Connell continued to up the stakes as the monster meetings continued throughout the summer. The largest so far was held on 15 August on the Hill of Tara where three quarters of a million of his supporters gathered. At Tara O'Connell said, 'Let every man who, if we had an Irish parliament would rather die than allow the Union to pass, lift up his hands.' But when O'Connell announced that the greatest monster meeting of them all was to be held at Clontarf, near Dublin, Peel decided to call his bluff. The day before the meeting was to be held, a proclamation was issued declaring it illegal and troops were sent to enforce the banning order. To avoid a bloodbath, O'Connell backed down and cancelled the meeting. A charge of conspiracy to incite disaffection was brought against O'Connell and other leaders and they were sentenced to imprisonment. After four months in prison, the sentence was quashed by the House of Lords but the O'Connell who emerged from prison was a beaten man.

After O'Connell's release from prison in September 1844, the demand for repeal was renewed, and although further great meetings were addressed by him, the enthusiasm of 1843 was never recaptured. In October 1844 he divided the Repeal Party when he stated his opinion that a federal system, in which Ireland would continue to be represented at Westminster, was preferable to simple Repeal of the Union. Weakened physically by overwork, disappointed by the failure of Repeal, worried over the disagreements with his supporters and suffering increasingly from ill health, O'Connell decided to go on a pilgrimage to Rome. When he reached Paris he was greeted by a large crowd of radicals who regarded him as the 'most successful champion of liberty and democracy in Europe'. O'Connell did not complete his journey to Rome; he died in Genoa on 15 May 1847. As he had requested, O'Connell's heart was buried in the Irish College in Rome (in a monument arranged by Charles Bianconi) and his body was interred in Glasnevin cemetery on 5 August 1847.

The younger wing of the Repeal Association, dubbed the 'Young Irelanders' by the English press, had become increasingly estranged from O'Connell during the final years of his leadership. Young Ireland attracted young members of the middle class whose aspirations went further than simple repeal. The movement aimed at a nationalism which would 'establish internal union and external independence.' Essentially, they sought a pluralist Ireland, while O'Connell's movement was overwhelmingly Catholic in character. The lead came from Thomas Davis, thirty-nine years old, son of an English army surgeon and an Irish mother; Charles Gavan Duffy a Catholic journalist; John Mitchel, a Belfast Protestant, and John Black Dillon from Mayo, a Catholic but a graduate from Trinity College. They rejected compromise with England and worked hard to create a concept of the Irish Nation which excluded landlords who were described as 'alien in race and religion'. An important element of the new nationalism was the revival of the Irish language. The movement's success stemmed largely from the popularity of its newspaper *The Nation* which had a print run of 12,000 copies and was widely distributed through Repeal reading rooms, claiming a readership of 250,000.

During the 1840s, the movement became increasingly divided as a second wave of recruits, including John Mitchel and Thomas Francis Meaghan, favoured revolution. In October 1847, at the height of the Great Famine, Mitchel urged tenants to withhold all agricultural produce for their own consumption and in December appealed to the peasants to arm themselves in defiance of the Government. The country, he later argued, was 'actually in a state of war — a war of "property" against poverty — a war of "law" against life'. His views were too extreme for many of his colleagues at *The Nation* so he founded his own

Young Irelander John Mitchel.

newspapers, *The United Irishman*, to promote his belief that, 'legal and constitutional agitation in Ireland is a delusion; that every man (except a born slave, who aspires only to beget slaves and die a slave) ought to have arms and to promote their use of them. That no good can come from an English Parliament.'

The rising, when it came, took place at the height of the famine when many were starving, dispirited and forced to migrate to the cities for work or as a prelude to emigration. It was led by an unlikely revolutionary.

William Smith O'Brien, the second son of Sir Edward O'Brien, 4th
Baronet of Dromoland Castle in County Clare, had entered Parliament as
a Conservative in 1826. His decision to join the Repeal Association in 1844
therefore caused something of a stir. He gave his reasons for such a change in
his political outlook at a banquet given in Limerick to celebrate his conversion to the Nationalist cause:

> The feelings of the Irish nation have been exasperated by every species of
> irritation and insult; every proposal tending to develop the resources of our
> industry, to raise the character and improve the condition of our population,
> has been discountenanced, distorted, or rejected. Ireland, instead of taking its
> place as an integral portion of the great empire which the valour of her sons
> has contributed to win, has been treated as a dependent tributary province;
> and at this moment, after forty-three years of nominal union, the affections
> of the two nations are so entirely alienated from each other, that England
> trusts for the maintenance of their connexion, not to the attachment of the
> Irish people, but to the bayonets which menace our bosoms, and the cannon
> which she has planted in all our strongholds.

The horrors of the famine and the French Revolution of 1848 combined to
urge O'Brien to insurrection. At the end of July 1848 he gathered a band of 500
peasants at Boylagh Common in Co. Tipperary. When the police arrived, they
withdrew to the farm of the widow McCormick. Unwisely, O'Brien sent them
home overnight to get rest and provisions, but most of his fledgling revolution-
aries never returned. As a result, the so-called 'Battle of Widow McCormick's
Cabbage Patch' at the end of July 1848 was little more than a skirmish, with a
small force of police firing their carbines from Mrs McCormick's farmhouse,
dispersing some fifty insurgents. Smith O'Brien had to suffer the further indignity of being abused by Mrs McCormick for the damage done to her land.
On his way to Dublin, under escort in a special train, he told an officer of the
Constabulary, 'I have played the game, and lost, and am ready to pay the penalty
of having failed. I hope that those who accompanied me may be dealt with in
clemency. I care not what happens to myself.' Before the sentence of death was
passed, he made a short speech in which he said, 'I am perfectly satisfied with
the consciousness that I have performed my duty to my country – that I have
done only that which it was, in my opinion, the duty of every Irishman to have
done.' The capital sentence was commuted to transportation for life and, after
a detention of about nine months at Spike Island in Cork Harbour, O'Brien
and several of his co-conspirators were sent from Kingstown to Tasmania in the
brig *Swift* on the 29 July 1849. In 1849 the remnants of the movement planned

The removal of Smith O'Brien. (John Mitchel, *Jail Journal*, 1854)

to kidnap Queen Victoria during her visit to Ireland and to hide her away in the mountains of County Dublin. The plan came to nothing however, and the would-be kidnappers had the added indignity of enduring the Queen's visit which proved to be an immense success.

The Young Irelanders' mantle was taken up by the Irish Republican Brotherhood, or the Fenian movement, which was founded simultaneously at Dublin and New York in 1858. Its leadership was mostly made up of middle-class intellectuals and at a local level they were drawn from school teachers, shopkeepers and soldiers. Many of its leaders, such as James Stephens and John O'Mahony, had been involved in the 1848 Rising. They had shared exile in Paris, where they mingled with the political exiles from many countries. This inspired them to establish a revolutionary society to work to overthrow British Rule in Ireland. They returned to Ireland in 1858 to make preparations.

The Fenians, like the United Irishmen, sought to make Irish Nationalism a non-sectarian movement. They prepared a secret military force, dedicated to the ideal of armed insurrection. Many members of the Catholic clergy considered them to be communists. The organisation

Cardinal Cullen.

The British Lion and the Irish Monkey. (*Punch*, 8 April 1848)

provoked a series of episcopal censures which made it clear that it was wrong to swear blind obedience to strangers who might not even be men of religion. It was also stated that the Fenian paper *The Irish People* preached socialism and disrespect for all ecclesiastical authority. Cardinal Paul Cullen in particular was outspoken in his opposition to Fenianism, declaring that they would 'destroy the faith of our people by circulating works like those of the impious Voltaire, to preach up socialism, to seize the property of those who have any, and to exterminate both the gentry of the country and the Catholic clergy.'

In fact, the Fenian leadership had no specific ideas about the nature of the Republic they were fighting for and had a less radical outlook than popularly supposed. Their sole objective was independence. Former Young Irelander John O'Leary called on England to cease governing Ireland and said, 'then I shall swear to be true to Ireland and the Queen or King of Ireland, even though that Queen or King should also happen to be Queen or King of England.' Charles J. Kingham, one of the most fervent anti-parliamentarian Fenians, would also have been willing to live under a constitutional monarchy in an Ireland separated from Britain. However, the official line, as laid down in *The Irish People*, was that a free Ireland would not be achieved by 'amiable and enlightened young men' imagining that 'they are surely regenerating their country, when

James Stephens Fenian.

they are pushing about in drawing room society … creating an Irish national literature, schools of Irish art, and things of this sort'. Such people were 'dilet-tante patriots, perhaps the greatest fools of all.'

Instead, British power was to be overthrown by force. Any delay would be dangerous; 'soon or never' were their watchwords. The organisation followed the American model: when fifty members had taken an oath of allegiance 'to the Irish Republic now virtually established', they constituted a local 'circle' placed under the command of an officer called a 'centre'. The movement was centralised under James Stephens who was self-designated 'Central Organiser of the Irish Republic'.

Dublin Fenian Rising prisoners at Mountjoy Prison, 1866. (*Illustrated London News*)

In spite of all episcopal efforts, the organisation built up a considerable following, including thousands of Irish soldiers serving in regiments stationed in Ireland. By 1865, thousands of small farmers and labourers had also been recruited. However, it differed from earlier national movements in that it drew much of its support from those who had emigrated to the USA or who had migrated to Britain in search of work. In New York the Fenians set up an Irish Senate and government-in-exile and maintained an army of Union Army veterans, some of whom invaded Canada in 1866. Much was made in the popular press of the presence of former soldiers returning to Ireland from the American Civil War. According to the *Cork Examiner* for 27 December 1865:

> The *Morning Herald* anticipates an outbreak in Ireland during the present winter. It grounds its belief on two reasons – one, that Ireland is now full of returned emigrants from America, who are reckless, but first-rate soldiers; the other, that it is generally supposed that there are at present at sea, on their way from America, steamers laden with arms and ammunition, and considerable numbers of fighting men.

When it came, two years later than anticipated in the popular press, the Fenian Rising of 4 March 1867 was no more successful than that of 1848. The government had been kept extremely well informed by John Corydon, a man who had infiltrated the highest ranks of the Brotherhood ensuring that most of the Fenian leaders were already in prison. This left a local band of insurgents confused and without direction. Every attempt over previous weeks to seize arms had been frustrated. In County Cork, rebels took the coastguard station of Knockadown and captured the police barracks in Ballyknockane, where they derailed the Dublin Express. Otherwise, all was failure. The constabulary dispersed groups of rebels in Drogheda's Potato Market, at Drumcliffe churchyard in Co Sligo, at Ballyhurst in Co Tipperary and repelled attacks on barracks at Ardagh and Kilmallock in Co Limerick. Dublin produced the largest Fenian turnout. Here several hundred men found themselves confronted at Tallaght by fourteen Constables under the command of Sub-Inspector Burke. The Fenians fired around fifty shots but not one of them found their mark. The police returned fire, wounding one man, and the insurgents scattered. The Irish Constabulary had been able to suppress the Fenian Rising without seeking the assistance of the military. Queen Victoria was so pleased that she renamed the force, the 'Royal Irish Constabulary'.

Sentences of death were commuted to terms of imprisonment with hard labour. There were, therefore, no martyrs for the cause in Ireland. It was a different matter in England. On 11 September 1867 police in Manchester arrested two men who were acting suspiciously in a doorway. One of them was none other than the head of the Fenian Brotherhood, Colonel Thomas Kelly. A week later around thirty Fenians ambushed an unescorted prison van taking Kelly and other convicts to Belle Vue Gaol. Inside, Police Sergeant Brett refused to open the van. A Fenian, Peter Rice, fired his revolver through the grille, mortally wounding the sergeant. A prisoner took the keys from the dying policeman and Kelly escaped.

Arrests followed and five faced trial for their lives. Four men were found guilty of murder: William Allen, Philip Larkin, Michael O'Brien and Edward Condon. None had fired the fatal shot but all openly confessed they were part of the rescue mission. All four made speeches from the dock. Michael O'Brien said, 'Look to Ireland; see the hundreds of thousands of its people in misery and want. See the virtuous, beautiful and industrious women who only a few years ago – aye and yet – are obliged to look at their children dying for want of food.' Edward Condon cried out, 'I have nothing to regret, to retract or take back. I can only say: God Save Ireland!' As *The Times* reported, the other prisoners all called out, 'in chorus and with great power: "God Save Ireland!"' Condon was given a last-minute reprieve because he was an American citizen. On the morning of 24 November 1867 Allen, Larkin and O'Brien were hanged before an immense crowd in Manchester, in what turned out to be the last public hanging in England.

Within a year of the Fenian Rising, the Liberal party returned to power. They were led by W.E. Gladstone, who had turned his thoughts to Ireland as a result of the failed rising. He was determined to resolve those issues which

Isaac Butt. (*Vanity Fare*, 2 May 1873)

he felt were at the heart of Irish dissatisfaction. During his first administration, 1868–74, two great measures of reform were brought into the statute books. Firstly, the Church Act of 1869 disestablished the Anglican Church. Secondly, the Land Act of 1870 was the first attempt at direct intervention in the land issue on behalf of the tenants.

Although Fenianism lingered on as a secret organisation, opposition to the Union in Ireland was taking a constitutional rather than revolutionary path. In 1870, the Home Rule movement was founded by Isaac Butt, a Donegal-born Protestant who had once held Unionist views. One of the leading barristers in the country, he had won the respect of many Irish Nationalists as a result of his brilliant legal defence of Young Irelander and Fenian prisoners. Permanently in debt, he was forced to concentrate on his legal work and was therefore little more than a part-time leader. Butt sought the creation of a subordinate parliament in Dublin which would have control of Irish affairs. Irish members of parliament would still represent their country at Westminster for Imperial issues. In May 1870 he put forward his views at a meeting held in Dublin from which sprang the Home Government Association, designed to mobilise public opinion behind the demand for an Irish Parliament. At the end of 1873 the Association was replaced by a new body, the Home Rule League. Butt regarded this body as a pressure group rather than a political party. When it was proposed that all Irish members elected on a Home Rule ticket should vote as the majority decided, Butt, along with the majority of members, rejected the proposal because it would destroy the independence of the individual member and risked alienating potential supporters at Westminster.

In the general election of 1874, the first to be fought after the Ballot Act of 1872 had established the secret ballot, the new party won more than half the Irish seats. Butt's attempts to persuade the major parties at Westminster to support Home Rule had little or no effect, and soon there arose within the Home Rule party a more extreme group who sought to take the offensive. Joseph Biggar and John O'Connor used the policy of obstructism to bring parliamentary business to a halt. This involved giving long speeches to delay passage of Irish coercion acts and to generally obstruct the business of the House in order to force the Liberals and Conservatives to negotiate with Irish nationalists. Obstructionism was used most effectively by a young cricket-loving Protestant landowner from county Wicklow, Charles Stewart Parnell. He was no great orator. Irish journalist and Nationalist MP, T.P. O'Connor later recalled:

> With no special powers of speech, except in moments of great passion and great emergency, Parnell was usually a dreary and a costive speaker. Yet you could see him there, standing up in the empty House, talking hour after hour

quite indifferent to the fact that there was nobody listening and nobody to listen; and the tall, thin figure, the impassive face, the inscrutable eyes, gave to this spectacle an almost uncanny look. An observation he made to me about the absence of any hearers while he droned out his dreary speeches hour after hour to the empty benches was very characteristic of the man. He said he rather liked an empty House; it gave him more time to think. Nobody ever cared less for the opinions of other people than Parnell.

Isaac Butt had no objection to Irish members arguing Irish cases in detail. However, he was concerned that deliberate obstruction would be counter-productive and would alienate potential supporters of the new Home Rule policy in the House of Commons. However, when the leadership of the movement passed to Parnell in 1880 it adopted a more radical agenda, leading many of the moderates to drift away and sit with the Liberals.

Parnell was convinced that the destruction of landlordism would lead to the overthrow of English power in Ireland. He told his audience at Galway on 24 October 1880 that, 'I would not have taken off my coat and gone to this work if I had not known that we were laying the foundation in this movement for the regeneration of our legislative independence'. His vision of the new Ireland was, to say the least, outlined in only the vaguest of terms. 'I feel confident that we shall kill the Irish landlord system', he told an audience in Cincinnati in 1880, 'and when we have we given Ireland to the people of Ireland we shall have laid the foundations upon which to build up our Irish nation'. In fact, he was only a Nationalist in the sense that he looked to a self-governing Ireland. He had little interest in the culture of Ireland. Tim Healy once declared that, 'Parnell in his heart cared little for the Irish.' Instead he fought for an Ireland which was run by the men of influence who lived in it. What made him an outstanding leader was the fact that he was able to keep the conflicting aims of the Fenians, Liberals, land agitators and Constitutionalists together with an iron discipline.

With a disciplined party behind him, he set about obtaining Home Rule. The General Election of 1885, fought on a new wider franchise which included the agricultural labourer, strengthened his party in the House of Commons and at the same time gave it the balance of power between the Liberals and Conservatives. In Ireland, Home Rulers had been returned for every seat outside Ulster and Dublin University. To Gladstone the result was decisive. He saw it as, 'the fixed desire of a nation, clearly and constitutionally expressed'. In August 1885, after the defeat of his second administration he became convinced of the need for some measure of Home Rule for Ireland. On his return to power in January 1886, he declared his determination to establish a devolved government in Dublin.

Gladstone's Home Rule bill of 1886 was a very moderate piece of legislation. There was to be an Irish legislature with an executive responsible to it,
but with a wide range of 'imperial' matters reserved from it including defence,
foreign and colonial affairs, custom and excise, trade and navigation. Although
the bill fell far short of legislative independence, it was welcomed by Parnell.
'We look upon the provisions of this bill as a final settlement of the Irish question and I believe that the Irish people have accepted it as a settlement.' He
added, 'Not a single dissentient voice has been raised against the bill by any
Irishman holding national opinions.'

Nevertheless, there were plenty who did oppose it in the belief that it
would destroy the unity of the British Empire and that is was a betrayal of
the Unionist and landlord class in Ireland. The strongest opposition to the
bill came from the Protestants of Ulster where drilling was already taking
place. A 'Monster Meeting of Conservatives and Orangemen' was held at
the Ulster Hall in Belfast on 22 February 1886 where the main speaker was
Conservative MP Lord Randolph Churchill, who told his cheering supporters that:

> If political parties and political leaders … should be so utterly lost to every
> feeling and dictate of honour and courage as to hand over coldly, and for
> the sake of purchasing a short and illusory parliamentary tranquillity, the
> lives and liberties of the loyalists of Ireland to their hereditary and most
> bitter foes, make no doubt on this point; Ulster at the proper moment will
> resort to the supreme arbitrament of force; *Ulster will fight, and Ulster will*
> *be right.*

A week before the meeting, Churchill had written to his friend Lord Justice
Fitzgibbon that if Gladstone, 'went for Home Rule, the Orange card would be
the one to play. Please God it may turn out the ace of trumps and not the two'.

Ulster had never been very fertile ground for the National Movements
which had dominated Irish political life throughout the nineteenth century.
T.P. O'Connor, writing in 1886, commented that, 'To the southern nationalist the north was chiefly known as the home of the most rabid religious and
political intolerance perhaps in the whole Christian world; it was designated
by the comprehensive title of the "Black North".' As early as 1825, Daniel
O'Connell had admitted to a House of Commons Committee on Ireland
that he had visited Ulster just once in his life and even then he had confined
his visit to the two most southern counties. When he later addressed an
Appeal Association meeting and dinner in Belfast in 1841, he travelled using
an alias and travelled two days early and by minor roads. In 1844, a German

traveller to Ireland, J G Kohl, noted that, although the Ulster Presbyterians showed leanings towards Republicanism, were anti-aristocratic and even anti-English, their bitterest enemies were southern Catholics. Kohl observed that O'Connell tended to avoid the town of Belfast during his tours of Ireland. He was told of one particular incident during his visit to Belfast:

Charles Stewart Parnell.

Shankill Road RIC barracks after the attack on it in June 1886. (Welch Collection, Ulster Museum)

I was told at Belfast that the great musician Liszt had the misfortune to be taken for O'Connell in the neighbourhood of that city, and was very near undergoing something extremely disagreeable that was intended for the agitator. As Liszt approached from Newry, in a handsome chaise drawn by four horses, and it was rumoured that the carriage contained a celebrated man, some of the Presbyterian rabble imagined it was O'Connell. They stopped the carriage, cut the traces, and compelled the eminent pianist to dismount, in order that they might wreak their anger against him in Irish fashion. They merely wished to duck him in a neighbouring pond, and then to advise him to return to his carriage, and to be off to the south of Ireland. It was some time before they discovered that, instead of the well-fed, old O'Connell, a young artist had fallen into their hands.

In the end, Gladstone's Home Rule Bill was defeated in the House of Commons by thirty votes, thanks to the opposition of the Conservatives and hostile members of the Liberal party led by Lord Hartington and Joseph Chamberlain. In the general election which was fought on the issue of Home Rule, Gladstone was heavily defeated.

An Irish Home Rule Bill would reach the House again under a short-lived Gladstone government in the early 1890s but Charles Stewart Parnell did not live to see it. In December 1889, William O'Shea, formerly one of Parnell's most loyal supporters, filed for divorce from his wife Katherine on the grounds of her adultery with Parnell. Kitty had in fact been Parnell's mistress for some years and Parnell was the father of three of her children. The scandal provoked a split in the party and Parnell was replaced as leader. He was politically sidelined and died in Brighton on 6 October 1891. Gladstone, on the other hand, despite being in his eighties, forced his Home Rule Bill through the House of Commons despite determined Unionist opposition. However, as expected, the Lords threw out the bill by 419 votes to 41. Gladstone wanted to call a general election on the issue but his cabinet would not support him. Dispirited by his failure to get Home Rule for Ireland, Gladstone retired in March 1894. He was replaced by Lord Rosebery who voiced his party's lack of commitment on the issue, 'there has been for a long time no enthusiasm for any measure.' In the election of 1895, the Conservatives returned to power and they were to remain there for the next decade. Prime Minister Lord Salisbury insisted that his administration would leave, 'Home Rule sleeping the sleep of the unjust'.

2

LIFE IN THE COUNTRYSIDE

The English visitor to the Irish countryside in the nineteenth century considered it a bleak and dreary place. They fretted over the absence of trees and hedgerows which were such a feature of the contemporary English landscape. To William Bilton, touring Ireland in the 1830s, the countryside had 'an unusually bare look in the eyes of an Englishman, and reminds him more of the interior of France than the smiling fields of England'. Irish-born lawyer Richard Lalor Sheil did little for the fledgling tourist industry in Ireland when he admitted in his *Memoirs* published in 1855 that:

> To those accustomed to English objects, the most fertile tracts look bare and barren. It is the country, but it has nothing rural about it; no luxuriant hedgerows, no shaded pathways, no cottages announcing by the neatness without, that cleanliness and comfort are to be found within; but one undiversified continuity of cheerless, stone-fences and parts of roadside hovels, with their typhus-beds piled up in front, and volumes of murky smoke forth issuing from the interior, where men and women, pigs and children, are enjoying the blessings of our glorious constitution.

What distressed many visitors was the almost total absence of trees. In many parts of Ireland it was more common to separate fields with an earthen bank, which discouraged the planting of trees. In other places, especially in the west, field boundaries were marked only by dry-stone walls which were evidence of the bitter struggle to clear the land. It was common for these stone walls to have no gate or obvious point of entry. According to the *Statistical Survey for County Clare*, 1808:

> In many parts of this country a gate is a rarity; when cattle are to be moved, a man takes down a yard or two of wall, and, when the cattle are in, builds

it up again; this, even with men of property, is the general practice twice
or oftener every day; I have seen, at several gentlemen's houses, dairy cows
and horses, that were moved twice every day, let in and out of the field in
this manner …

Frenchman Paschal Grousset, declared that trees were for the wealthy alone:

> The most striking thing on a first sight of the Irish landscape is the total
> absence of trees of any kind. They are only seen in private parks. As far as the
> eye can see the plains spread in gentle undulations, covered with grass and
> intersected with stone walls; no single oak, elm, or shrub ever comes to break
> its monotony. The tree has become a lordly ensign. Whenever one sees it one
> may be certain the landlord's mansion is not far.

The barren nature of the countryside was enlivened by the mansions of the
great land owners. Traditionally referred to as 'big houses', their scale and
opulence reflected the often colossal scale of these great estates. By the 1870s
more than half the land was owned by fewer than 1,000 major landlords.
The major landowners managed great estates which were often distributed
through two or three counties; the Marquis of Downshire had 115,000 acres

Maria Edgeworth's House. (Richard Lovett, *Irish Pictures Drawn with Pen and Pencil*,
1888)

Maria Edgeworth Library. (Richard Lovett, *Irish Pictures Drawn with Pen and Pencil*, 1888)

in Antrim, Down, Kildare, King's County and Wicklow; Lord Landsdowne owned 120,000 acres in Counties Dublin, Kerry, Limerick, Meath and Queen's; and the Marquess of Conyngham owned more than 156,000 acres in Clare, Donegal and Meath.

Visitors to Ireland were struck by the great mansion houses like Powerscourt, Castletown and Castle Coole with their lofty architecture and elegant interiors. The grandeur of these buildings was in marked contrast to the hovels of the vast majority of rural dwellers. Maria Edgeworth, best selling author of *Castle Rackrent*, described the newly refurbished Pakenham Hall in 1821:

> Lord Longford has finished and furnished his castle which is now really a mansion fit for a nobleman of his fortune. The furniture is neither gothic nor Chinese nor gaudy nor frail but substantially handsome and suitable in all its parts – the library scarlet and black with some red morocco cushioned chairs … The furniture in the drawing room a kind of old china pattern like an old gown of Aunt Mary's – a delightful abundance of sofas and cushions and chairs and tables of all sorts and sizes.

Another celebrated chronicler of Irish life, Edith Somerville, remembered her grandmother's house, Drishane House in County Cork:

Its rooms are lofty, and their proportions pleasant. Of these, the first that may be dealt with is the drawing-room, a place of great sanctity, wherein the foot of child never trod save by special invitation (or command, which came to the same thing). Its wall-paper was white, spaced into large diamonds with a Greek pattern of gold and it shone like satin. It was less dashing in design than the paper of the inner hall and the staircase, whose pattern was of endless ladders of large blue and orange flowers (tropic, one believed them to be) that raged from the bottom of the house to the top, but the drawing-room was devoted to the ladies, and in it dash gave way to refinement. Portraits of ancestresses hung round it, close to the ceiling, according to the practice of those domestic picture-hangers who hold no brief for Art. Ancestors were relegated to the dinning-room, as being, I suppose, a more suitable environment for the thirstier sex.

These great houses with huge households were often remote and required great organisational skills. Letters and household accounts reveal an endless list of goods that had to be trundled down to the estate by cart. The main household requirements were normally provided by the estate: peat or wood for heating, meat and game from the farm and woods, vegetables and fruit from the walled gardens. J.M. Callwell recalled in her *Old Irish Life* (1912):

> Our household allowance was a sheep every week and a bullock once a month, all that could not be eaten fresh being salted down in huge stone pickling-troughs. In addition the poultry-yard had its tribes of feathered fowl, farther afield rabbits multiplied in a manner devastating to the young plantations, trout abounded in the lake, so did game in its season. Fuel we had free, too, for we were surrounded by turf-bogs – a very important matter, indeed, in all Irish households in those days, for except in the towns near the coast coal was rarely burnt.

Some landowners located their houses amidst hundreds of acres of parkland and gardens, building high demesne walls or surrounding their houses with woodland, and so distanced themselves from the local community. A buffer of employees, including agents, stewards and bailiffs, helped maintain this distance. Landlords were nevertheless the main source of employment in the region: estate workers, servants, blacksmiths and stonemasons all looked to the local landowner for work. Farm work, the cultivation of extensive and often elaborate gardens and the preservation of game provided a good deal of employment on demesnes as at Powerscourt, where up to fifty men were employed at high season. Demesne employees included gardeners, grooms, coachmen, agricul-

Powerscourt House. (Richard Lovett, *Irish Pictures Drawn with Pen and Pencil*, 1888)

Powerscourt, Wicklow.

tural labourers, herds, shepherds, gamekeepers, yardmen, blacksmiths, foresters, carpenters, masons and plasterers. It was the job of the steward to supervise the activities of demesne employees who were often members of the same family and worked as retainers for generations.

Many of this great army of employees and retainers took great pride in their association with the local landlord. Elizabeth Charlotte in her *Letters from Ireland,* 1837, was amused by the attitude of her driver as she approached Tollymore House, County Down, the residence of Lord Roden:

> I shall not forget the smile with which the poor driver turned his head to look at me, when a rapturous exclamation burst from my lips; and while we proceeded along a beautiful road, edged with handsome cottages, he remarked, 'Lord Roden's village': then, passing a most respectable dwelling, with its range of stabling, he added, 'Lord Roden's inn'; and wheeling his horses to the right, where a very fine gateway and picturesque lodge marked the entrance, he almost triumphantly concluded, 'Lord Roden's park!'

The more philanthropic landowners took an active roll in the amelioration of poverty in the neighbouring area. William Makepeace Thackeray noted in the 1840s, after a visit to a gentleman's estate on his way between Carlow and Waterford:

> several men and women appeared sauntering in the grounds, and as the master came up, asked for work, or sixpence, or told a story of want. There are lodge-gates at both ends of the demesne; but it appears the good-natured practice of the country admits a beggar as well as any other visitor. To a couple our landlord gave money, to another a little job of work; another he sent roughly out of the premises: and I could judge thus what a continual tax upon the Irish gentleman these travelling paupers must be, of whom his ground is never free.

Absentee landlords, on the other hand, were heavily criticised throughout the nineteenth century. Before 1845 an estimated 33 per cent to 50 per cent of Irish landowners were absentees, although a substantial number of these owned more than one estate and when living on one became effectively absentee on all the others. They were, nevertheless, regularly condemned in the press and in travel accounts of the period. Thomas Campbell Foster, in his *Letters on the Condition of the People of Ireland* (1846), was highly critical of the absentee Marquis of Conyngham after a visit to his estate in Glenties, County Donegal:

Rent Day.

Once in the course of his life – two years ago – the Marquis of Conyngham
visited this estate for a few days. His chief agent, Mr. Benbow, usually comes
once a year, and the sub-agents visit the tenants every half year to collect
their rents. At short periods of a few years, the farms are visited to see what
increased rent they will bear, and this is the extent of the acquaintance of
the Marquis of Conyngham with his tenants. The nobleman, himself, bears
the character of a kind-heated, generous man – fond of yachting and amusement, and having an excessive distaste for every kind of business or trouble.
From one end of his large estate here to the other, nothing is to be found but
poverty, misery, wretched cultivation, and infinite subdivision of land. There
are no gentry, no middle class – all are poor – wretchedly poor. Every shilling
the tenants can raise from their half-cultivated land is paid in rent, whilst the
people subsist for the most part on potatoes and water.

Absenteeism did not necessarily mean estates were neglected or tenants
exploited. Many estates were effectively run by land stewards or agents. On the
other hand, some of the most infamous landlords who were most unpopular
with tenants were resident and took a very personal interest in rent and eviction. Ironically, the fiercest critics of absentees for much of the century were
not farmers or tenants but resident landlords who felt that they were unfairly
expected to shoulder unpalatable and time-consuming local, social and political responsibilities for which they received no reward and scant recognition.

The land agent on most estates was the landlord's representative, responsible for the day-to-day running of the estate. Their duties varied, but included collecting rents, setting leases, valuing property and generally enforcing the landlord's property rights. During elections, an agent might act for this employer's candidate. They frequently acted as justices of the peace and Poor Law guardians. Eighteenth-century agents were often members of the minor gentry but by the nineteenth century they had acquired a greater degree of professionalism. French journalist Paschal Grousset was impressed by the role of the agent:

> He is neither a notary, nor a steward, and yet he partakes of both, being the intermediary between the landlord and tenant. It is he that draws up the leases and settlements; he who receives the rents, who sends out summons, who signs every six months the cheque impatiently expected by the landlord; he who represents him at law, he who negotiates his loans, mortgages, cessions of income, and all other banking operations. In a word, he is the landlord's prime minister, the person who takes on his shoulders all the management of his affairs, and reduces his profession to the agreeable function of spending money.

Next down the social scale came the tenant farmers and their families who accounted for half the rural population, numbering about 500,000 in the 1860s. They leased their land from the landlords and worked full-time on their farm with the help of their immediate family and hired labourers. As a group they were more varied than the landlords; their holdings ranged from a few acres to large graziers such as Edward Delany of Woodtown who held 500 acres in County Meath. Usually referred to locally as 'respectable', when commentators wished to distinguish between them and the average tenant who held their land from year to year, one observer in the 1840s defined them as having 'very comfortable and independent circumstances … they settle their sons well and give large portions [dowries] to their daughters on their marriage'.

These better-off farmers also employed servants and, according to John Gamble, who stayed on one such farm in 1812, the servant enjoyed a better life than the surrounding peasantry:

> After the churning was finished, the servants and labourers were set down to their dinner at the kitchen table. They had a most abundant one. It consisted of milk, butter, potatoes, and greens, pounded together, and oaten cake. This is Wednesday, or else, in addition to the milk and butter, they would have had bacon, or hung beef. Wednesdays and Fridays are perpetual fasts of the church of Rome, and no luxury or dainty could tempt the poor Irish peasant to eat flesh-meat, on either of those days, or during the whole course of Lent. Admirable forbearance!

Most tenants had a yearly tenancy and could be evicted with only six months' notice to quit; rents could be increased annually and evicted tenants had no right to compensation for improvements. The Ulster Custom in the north left the tenants in a much better position than those in the other provinces. It was a practice by which a tenant paying rent to his landlord should not be evicted without being paid by the incoming tenant, or by the landlord, the full marketable price of his interest in the farm, this interest being the value of his own improvements, and those inherited from his ancestors. This custom ensured that the landlord could not raise the rent as the tenant effected improvements in his holding. Englishman John Gough, who visited Ireland in 1813-14, noted the difference in attitude of tenants in the north, 'How very different is the situation of the common people in Ulster province, though living under the same government, and subject to the very same laws. There, the poorest man, looking upon himself as a man, would not tamely submit to unmerited insult from anyone.'

Further down the social scale was the cottier tenant who worked for a landlord and lived in cottages provided by him on his estate. If employment was regular these were the most secure of their class and their income, in conjunction with the sale of a calf or a pig, left the family with a small cash surplus after rent had been allowed for. There were others, however, who rented a plot for cash and sought employment from any source available. These were the worst-off cottiers. They paid inflated rents for an acre or half-acre of potato ground and, unlike other cottiers who employers provided grazing for a cow at a moderate charge, they had to buy milk from farmers in the locality.

The largest group found in the countryside, and at the bottom of the social scale, was agricultural labourers who walked the roads in search of work. If the labourer could write he kept his accounts in writing, but if he was unable to write he kept a tally – a stick split up the middle – one part being kept by the labourer and the other by the farmer. For everyday worked a notch or stroke was put on each stick. If at the end the tallies did not agree the labourer could go to the magistrate to recover his wages. Generally the labourer was reluctant to do this; it cost sixpence and could lose the labourer time spent working.

The poor labourer walking the roads in search of work was a common sight until the late nineteenth century. The first of these migrants made their appearance in the spring, when the ground was being broken up for tillage. At the end of the season he took his pay and set off again to his own place, to dig potatoes or save his own little crop. In their absence their families frequently lived by begging, especially during the 'hungry months' or 'meal months' of June and July after the year's stock of potatoes had been used up and before the new ones became available. According to *The First Report from His Majesty's*

A potato dinner. (*Pictorial Times*, 28 February 1846)

Commissioners for Inquiring into the Condition of the Poorer Classes in Ireland, published in 1835, in the parish of Abbey and Oughtmanagh, County Clare:

> Of the unemployed months, July is by far the severest for the working man. His stock of con-acre potatoes is then nearly exhausted, and the price of potatoes is then at the highest; and if the number of his meals suffer no reduction, they become more scanty, and he is obliged to do without the addition even of a little milk.

'As it is,' Sergeant Patrick Norton told the Commissioners, 'a miracle to me, who am accustomed to England, how the most of them live at all; and yet,' he said, 'except in peculiarly scarce seasons, neither their wives nor children are to be seen begging; at least openly. They may go to a neighbour's to borrow a lock of potatoes, but nothing more.'

Labourer and cottier shared a potato diet. In his *Survey of Kilkenny*, published in 1802, William Tighe observed:

> Potatoes, with milk, as often as it can be procured, form almost the whole of the food of the poorer classes in this parish: before the introduction of the kind called the apple potato, a great portion of the sustenance of the poor here, consisted of oaten bread and milk; from April to August barley bread was sometimes used, and in the hilly parts of the parish, rye-bread: but since the cultivation of the apple potatoes have become general, the

poor continue to eat them until the new potatoes come in. Before their introduction, the cottagers frequently sowed beans and other suculent vegetables, and had little plots somewhat like a small kitchen garden, at the rear of their cabins, but the apple potato has superseded every thing of this sort.

Sidney Godolphin Osborne, who visited Ireland at the height of the Famine, condemned landlords for their support for this dependence on the potato. In his *Gleanings from the West of Ireland*, published in 1850, he declared:

> If Providence had not blighted the potato, I do not believe the West of Ireland would have seen the landlords so bent on the destruction of the small holding class. So long as 'Pat's' lazy bed of potatoes, enabled him to pay the Rack-sent, which kept up the old style of Irish living, of the agents at home, and of the absent landlord; a style notorious for its extravagance; Pat might have slept and bred as much as he liked; the more mouths, the more potatoes would be wanted – the more competition for potato land; such competition was the very soul of rack-rent.

The one-room mud cabins they lived in accounted in 1841 for 40 per cent of the houses in Ireland. Furniture in these mud cabins usually consisted of a bed of straw, a crude table and stool and a few cooking utensils. Henry David Inglis left an account of the mud cabins he visited in the Wicklow Mountains in his *Ireland in 1834*. 'It was neither air nor water tight; and the floor was extremely damp. The furniture consisted of a small bedstead, with very scanty bedding, a wooden bench, and one iron pot; the embers of some furze burnt on the floor; and there was neither chimney nor window.' The *Dublin Penny Journal*, 1833, complained:

> There is nothing in Ireland that strikes the eye of a non-native traveller, so much as the misery – the squalid misery of the habitation of our people. The tottering, crumbling, mud walls – the ragged, furrowed, and half rotten thatch – the miserable basket-shaped orifice that answers as a chimney – the window, with its broken panes stuffed with a wisp of straw, or some rags, filthy and nasty – the dunghill before the un-fitting door, which the pig has broken; altogether the erection is one which no unaccustomed eye can repose on without disgust and pity; and hard is the heart, and worthless the man, who would not desire to give any fellow-creature a better home and sojourn in this vale of sorrow and trial, more consonant to a thinking and immortal being.

To those who managed to keep their families from destitution, the death of the principal breadwinner could bring about a sudden decline in a family's fortunes. The Commissioners who were inquiring into the conditions of the poorer classes in the parish of Abbey and Oughtmanagh in the 1830s were told:

> that it was only necessary that the father of a family among the labouring classes should die, in order that his children should be reduced to a state of destitution fully equal to that of an infant deserted by its parents; so much so, that children whose mothers alone survive, are always considered and styled orphans.

Sometimes a child taken under the roof of a peasant who was too poor to give him any food was forced to beg. The Commissioners encountered a small boy of eight years on the road, carrying a bag containing a few small potatoes. When questioned, he told the Commissioners that 'his father and mother were dead, and that he and his two sisters, younger than himself, were living with a poor man in the next parish, and that he was obliged each day to go about collecting potatoes for himself and his sisters'. The law specified that a cess shall be levied only for deserted children, 'but', observed one of the witnesses, 'it is all the same, as neither the one nor the other are provided for here.'

The old fared little better, as they were dependent upon the generosity of their families for survival. The Commissioners found:

> Where there is no property in question, the aged parent generally takes up his abode with his son or daughter, and, on the whole, these poor people treat their parents much better, and scarcely any instances were known, in that part of the country, of the parents of labourers being obliged to beg publicly; in fact, the poorer the people were, the greater seemed to be the anxiety to preserve the respectability of their families. The support of the aged parents presses very heavily on the children; and many cannot afford the little indulgences which old age requires, without depriving themselves of absolute necessaries.

In the countryside, women played a vital role in bringing in extra money to hard-pressed households. Many were employed in the textile industry, working from their homes on the outworking system which was badly paid compared to those employed in the factories. They were also a very visible presence in the fields as noted by Harriet Martineau in 1852:

we observe women working almost everywhere. In the flax-fields there are more women than men pulling and steeping. In the potato-fields it is often the women who are saving the remnant of the crop. In the harvest-fields there are as many women as men reaping and binding. In the bog, it is the women who, at half wages, set up, and turn, and help to stack the peat – not only for household use, but for sale, and in the service of the Irish Peat Company.

There was a dramatic change in the range of agricultural work available to women by the end of the nineteenth century. Changing land-usage patterns, the shift from tillage to dairying, increased stock rearing which was less labour intensive, growing levels of mechanisation and the coming of the creameries, which removed butter-making from the home, all took their toll on women's agricultural opportunities by the end of the nineteenth century, forcing many into the cities in search of work.

Peat cutting. (Richard Lovett, *Irish Pictures Drawn with Pen and Pencil*, 1888)

Dress varied even within the various elements of rural society. The better-off farmer wore kneebritches, waistcoat, shirt and cravat, tailcoat and sturdy boots. His wife wore a cloak which covered a bodice, 'midi'-skirt and shift. The lower grades had generally the same cut of clothes, but they were more ragged and patched. Few of the labourers had overcoats and the women and children generally went barefoot. Among the very poor, clothing was little better than rags. Dr John Forbes condemned men in the 1850s for their:

> abominable habit, so long prevalent among the poor in Ireland, of wearing the cast-off clothes of others. This habit, originating, no doubt, in poverty, has, I think, been carried much further than was absolutely necessary, merely because it had become a habit. I think it must be beginning to wear out, as I observe that a fair proportion of the boys and young men show themselves, as least on Sundays, in jackets and short coats, evidently originals … Nothing could convey to a stranger a stronger impression of wretchedness and untidiness, than this vicarious costume of the Irish, disfiguring at once to the person of the wearers, and calling forth in the mind of the observer the most disagreeable associations. Even when not in holes, as they too often are, those long-tailed coasts almost touching the ground, and those shapeless breeches with their gaping knee-bands sagging below the calf of the leg, are the very emblems and ensigns of beggary and degradation.

As with all aspects of Victorian life there was a great gulf between those in want and those who had money to spare. At Ballinrobe, in 1862, Henry Coulter noted while he was in town on a holy day, the place was thronged with people:

> The shops were thronged to excess; the main street was almost impassable from the denseness of the crowd; and, judging from the comfortable appearance and cheerful countenances of the people, no one would suspect that there was any prospect of distress in the districts from which this well-clad and orderly multitude had come.

Although travel accounts in Ireland portray the Irish peasantry as stoic and content, contemporary newspapers paint a picture of rural Ireland as seething with discontent. For the tenant farmer two issues were a source of grievance – tithe and rents. The tithe, which nominally earmarked one-tenth of the produce of the land for the maintenance of the established clergy, was payable in kind such as the tenth cow or sheep. But in many parts of Ireland, payment was made in cash. According to the *Statistical Survey of Cork,* published in 1810:

The usual mode is to have them valued, previous to the harvest and to appoint days of meeting with the parishioners, for the purpose of letting them. Small tithes, or (as they are commonly called) small dies, viz, those of wool, lambs, & c. are for the most part relinquished, potatoes, corn, and hay being the titheable articles. Flax, cultivated extensively only in the south-west quarter, is commonly rated at four shillings per peck for the seed sowed. In some parts of the same district hay, unless the quantity be considerable, is not tithed. The prices of valuation vary, according to circumstances and situation, from six to fourteen shillings for potatoes; from six to twelve for wheat and barley; and from three to six for hay and oats.

The tithe was paid half-yearly in November and May, but was difficult to collect and uneven in its levy. Tithe was generally collected by a tithe-proctor rather than by the incumbent clergyman. The clergyman received a fixed sum and the excess was retained by the proctor who had therefore strong motivation to exact every last penny for himself. According to the *Statistical Account for County Clare*, published in 1808:

> The rates of tithe vary according to the disposition of the clergyman or his tithe-proctor, and are a tolerable barometer of the love or dislike of his parishioners; where they are higher than customary, you may be certain of finding a turbulent divine, who will have his rights, regardless whether he is liked or disliked, or, if he is a non-resident, his proctor is of the same way of thinking. If, on the contrary, they are moderately exacted, the love and respect of his neighbours follow of course.

Inevitably, the tithe proctor was unpopular in local communities. As more peasants crowded the land, resistance to the payment of tithe increased. Agrarian secret societies sprang into being, and their efforts to prevent the collection of tithes led to widespread intimidation and violence. Eventually the government gave way to popular pressure and introduced the Tithe Rent Charge Act in 1838 which reduced by 25 per cent the tithe payment and transferred payment from the tenant to the landowner.

Rents were usually paid half-yearly: the county rents were due on 1 May and 1 November while town leases were often due on 25 March (old New Year's Day known as Lady Day or the Annunciation of the Blessed Virgin Mary) and 29 September (Michaelmas). Tenants, cottiers and agricultural labourers who had difficulty paying their rents faced the constant threat of eviction. Evictions are popularly associated with the Great Famine, but they took place in large numbers throughout the nineteenth century and indeed the latter half of the

Farm labourers. (Attributed to Augusta Crofton, 1857)

eighteenth century is peppered with accounts of tenants being ejected from their homes.

In the years before the Great Famine, landlords used the threat of eviction to manage the tenants on their estates. When landlords intervened in family disputes, or in disputes between tenants, the notice to quit was their sanction – they could use it to threaten poachers, trespassers, drunkards, bad farmers, wife-beaters. Many used the process in moderation; others abused the system. Lord Leitrim, for example, served all his tenants annually with notices to quit and kept them in a permanent state of insecurity.

Landowners were greatly assisted by the fact that the process of eviction before the Land Act of 1879 was simple and quick. It usually took the form of threats of eviction before notices to quit were served on the tenants. If a landlord wished to eject for non-payment, the tenant was served with a process stating the amount of rent and costs due; if he wanted to get rid of a tenant who was not in arrears, he had to give six months' notice to quit, followed by a process for overholding. Both processes summoned the tenant to appear in court to show why he had not paid his rent or given up his holding. The difference between them was impor-tant: the ejectment for non-payment could be stopped by the tenant paying his arrears and costs; the ejectment for overholding could be stopped only if the landlord gave up the case or the tenant got out.

Finally eviction, the forcible removal of the tenant by the sub-sheriff, was carried out or assisted if necessary by the constabulary. This process could take place only with the approval of a court. If the court decided in the landlord's favour, he was given an ejectment decree, which was an order to the sheriff to give the landlord possession of the holding. The decree had to be executed within a certain period; it could not he held indefinitely as a threat to the tenant. It had to be executed on a weekday between 9am and 3pm. It could not, after 1848, be executed on Christmas Day or Good Friday. The landlord or his agent had to inform the relieving officer at least forty-eight hours before the eviction took place; failure to do so could lead to a fine of £20. The amount of force that could be used was strictly regulated. It was, for example, a misdemeanour to unroof a house while it was still occupied. A tenant evicted for non-payment had six months in which to redeem his holding by paying arrears and costs.

Many landowners cared little for the niceties of the law, and their willingness to use force to evict tenants became increasingly marked during the Great Famine. The system of poor relief introduced into Ireland in 1838 was financed out of local rates and, as the workhouses began to fill up with the sick and destitute, the chief costs fell upon the landlords, many of whom were already burdened with debt. Their income was also badly affected by the non-payment of rents and they were forced to sell their estates often heavily mortgaged. During the 1850s more than 5 million acres, almost a quarter of the land in Ireland, passed into the hands of new landlords, many of whom were wealthy speculators. The more progressive of these saw eviction as a necessary first step to improving land management on their estates.

It is impossible to be certain how many people were evicted during the years of the Famine and its immediate aftermath. The police began to keep an official tally in 1849 and they recorded a total of nearly 250,000 persons as formally and permanently evicted from their holdings between 1849 and 1854. This figure does not take into account illegal evictions and voluntary surrender of land. If we were to guess at the equivalent number for 1846-8 and to include the countless thousands pressured into involuntary surrenders during the whole period, the resulting figure would almost certainly exceed half a million people.

Many landlords and their agents used physical force or heavy-handed pressure to bring about evictions. It was the practice to level or burn the affected dwellings there and then, as soon as the tenants' effects had been removed. This was frequently carried out in front of a large number of spectators and, as the century progressed, ladies and gentlemen of the press. 'Ordinary evictions are commonplace affairs, but those which are carried out at the price of a regular battle are worth going to see' noted Anne de Bovet, a French journalist who came to Ireland in the 1870s to report on the Land War. She was fascinated by the excitement an eviction could create in the locality:

The whole apparatus of the law is brought into play – police, infantry, and cavalry. Barricading themselves in their houses, the inhabitants launch from the windows stones, broken pots, hot oil, and boiling water. To break in the doors a sort of battering ram is employed, the walls are demolished stone by stone, men, women and children are dragged forth by main force, the movables are turned out, the doors and windows closed with plants, and sometimes the roof itself taken off to render the tenement uninhabitable. All this goes on amid the execrations of a yelling crowd, which an agitator or the priest of the parish inflames with well understood exhortations to abstain from violence.

As the nineteenth century progressed, rural violence became increasingly marked as the rural population began to resist eviction. Among the landlords killed was Lord Mountmorris, who was murdered in September 1880 near his residence, Ebor Hall, in County Galway. He had a small estate with fifteen tenants with whom he had a poor relationship, having shortly before his death obtained ejectment decrees against two of them. Even more unpopular was William Clements, 3rd Lord Leitrim, who owned property amounting to 94,535 acres, including an estate of 54,352 acres in north Donegal, who was murdered on 2 April 1878. His arrogance and brutality alienated him even from members of his own class. He had, for example, removed all the tenants of Rawros to build his castle at Manorvaughan and those at Cratlagh to plant a vista of trees. He had a chapel pulled down with the aid of crowbar men and forced a farmer keeping goats against the rules to kill them on the spot before his eyes. The *Manchester Guardian* of 4 April 1878 in condemning the murder had to concede:

It is unfortunately impossible to deny that Lord Leitrim was accustomed to think far more of his own rights than of what was due to his tenants. He was in a state of constant warfare with the people on his extensive property and he drew upon himself increased odium from the personal part he took in the work of eviction. We are told, for example, that he 'usually appeared as his own counsel and witness in ejectment cases' – a practice which could hardly fail to intensify the popular resentment against him. Whatever may be said of him, he was certainly unfortunate in his relations to tenantry; but it is only in Ireland that this circumstance would be pleaded as an extenuation of the dreadful crime which has been committed.

Shortly after his murder Margaret Dixon McDougall, author of *The Letters of 'Norah' on her Tour Through Ireland* (1882) was driven over the Leitrim's estate and found:

The murdered Earl has left a woeful memory of himself all over the country side. He must have had as many curses breathed against him as there are leaves on the trees, if what respectable people who dare speak of his doings say of him be true, which it undoubtedly is. Godly people of Scottish descent, Covenanters and Presbyterians, who would not have harmed a hair of his head for worlds, have again and again lifted their hands to heaven and cried. 'How long, Lord, are we to endure the cruelty of this man?'

In an attempt to address the land issue, Gladstone introduced a bill to bring about a radical reform through the Irish land system. Its leading feature was a Land Commission to adjudicate rents, and therefore to establish the principle of dual ownership of land, by both owners and tenants, into the law. The new Act also guaranteed the tenant fixity of tenure, provided he paid the rent and gave him the right to sell his holding together with any improvements he had made to it, to an incoming tenant. Although it did not go far enough for many, it worked well. The rents fixed by the land courts were reasonable and the return of better potato harvests meant that the crisis on the land was temporarily easing. On the other hand, landlords experienced reductions in rent which averaging around 20 per cent. As one contemporary observer noted, there was an unpleasant irony to this. 'The landlords who have suffered least have probably been those who simplified their properties by wholesale evictions'.

A series of Land Acts followed, culminating in the 1903 Act, popularly known as the Wyndam Act, which offered the landlords a 12 per cent bonus in addition to the agreed price if they agreed to sell out their entire estate. The act also introduced the principle of sale of the whole estate, with tenants agreeing to common terms, rather than the piecemeal sale of holdings. Provision was also made for the purchase of estates by the Land Commission and the resale of untenanted lands to uneconomic holders or evicted tenants. The act was popular with tenants because it guaranteed annual repayments lower than existing rents.

Therefore, by the beginning of the twentieth century, government legislation had brought about in Ireland a complete revolution in land ownership. Within a generation the position of the landlords in Ireland had been altered as the land passed into the hands of the former tenants. 'The Act undid the confiscations of James I, Cromwell, and William III', as Nationalist MP Tim Healy, a supporter of the Wyndam Act, remarked. Between 1870 and 1933 tenants in what is now the Republic of Ireland bought out 450,000 holdings, a total of 15 million acres out of 17 million. The land question had, at last, been removed from Irish politics.

3

LIFE IN THE TOWNS

Ireland remained a predominately rural society throughout the nineteenth century. The 1841 census states that one fifth of the population of Ireland were town-dwellers but this is misleading because it included any settlement exceeding twenty houses. Only five centres, Dublin, Cork, Belfast, Limerick and Waterford, had more than 20,000 inhabitants. Most other towns were little known outside their immediate hinterland as Henry Inglis confessed in his *Ireland in 1834*, 'There are only some few we ever hear of. Leaving Cork, Waterford, Limerick, and Belfast out of the list, less I think is known of the other towns, unless by the gentlemen of the army, than of the same class of towns in the continent.'

For most visitors Dublin remained the first port of call on their Irish odyssey. And yet the nineteenth century was often traumatic for the Irish capital. Dublin would begin the century by losing its Parliament and end it under threat from Belfast, its industrial rival in the north for the title of Ireland's largest city. The sale in 1802 of the buildings of the late Parliament House to the Bank of Ireland emphasised the city's loss of prestige. Yet it remained an administrative, military and cultural capital, noted for its public buildings. Its faded grandeur lingered on and impressed visitors to the city throughout the nineteenth century. Kohl considered Dublin uncharacteristic of the rest of the country:

Dublin is, in its exterior, an entirely English city. Except its miserably poor, filthy suburbs, and its lanes so thickly peopled with beggars, it possesses nothing which the great English cities do not possess, and which it has not received from the other side of the Channel. The private houses of the wealthy are just as small, neat, unornamented, and precisely of the same cut and design, as private houses in all English towns. And the public buildings are just as rich in ornaments and columns, as full of rotundas, colonnades,

and porticos, as the public buildings of English cities, like the houses of
Pericles on the Acropolis of Athens ... Nelson's Pillar (a lofty, handsome
column) stands in the middle of Sackville-street, the most splendid street
in Dublin; whilst Wellington Testimonials and King George's Statues are
as plentiful in the city as in English towns. Trinity College (the Dublin
University) has its beautiful walled-in garden, like the Oxford colleges; and
the Castle, the seat of the Viceroy, is a repetition of many similar castles to
be found in England. You must not however imagine, because you are now
in a Catholic country, that this, its capital, possesses anything peculiar in the
way of old churches and cloisters, splendid Catholic cathedrals, or many-
coloured chapels at the street corners. One remarks as little of Catholicism
in Dublin as of Protestantism in Prague – just as little as in all the other
towns of the British empire.

William Makepeace Thackeray's first impressions of Dublin was that the
'entrance to the capital is very handsome. There is no bustle and throng
of carriages, as in London; but you pass by numerous rows of neat houses,
fronted with gardens and adorned with all sorts of gay-looking creepers.'
Henry D Inglis, who visited the Irish capital in 1834, was also struck by the
grandeur of the city:

> A stranger arriving in Dublin in Spring, as I did, will be struck, even less
> by the architectural beauty of the city, than by other kinds of splendour:
> I allude to the indulgences of luxury, and the apparent proofs of wealth that
> are everywhere thrust upon the eye – the numerous private vehicles that fill
> the streets, and even blockade many of them; the magnificent shops for the
> sale of articles of luxury and taste, at the doors of which, in Grafton Street, I
> have counted upwards of twenty handsome equipages; and in certain quarters
> of the city, the number of splendid houses, and 'legion' of liveried servants.

The other side of Dublin life also made an impression on Henry Inglis as he
stayed in a house in Kildare Street which was exactly opposite to the Royal
Dublin Society, then exhibiting a cattle show:

> After the cattle had been fed, the half-eaten turnips became the prerequisite
> of the crowd of ragged boys and girls without. Many and fierce were the
> scrambles for these precious relics; and a half-gnawed turnip, once secured,
> was guarded with the most vigilant jealousy, and was lent for a mouthful to
> another longing tatterdemalion, as much apparently as an act of extraordi-
> nary favour, as if the root had been a pineapple.

Jonathan Binns, in his *Miseries and Beauties of Ireland*, 1837, acknowledged that while London was also a city of contrasts, in Dublin the contrast between rich and poor was more immediately obvious:

> Dublin is indeed a fine city; but it is a city of lamentable contrasts. If the stranger be forcibly struck by the number and magnificence of the public buildings, and the general beauty of some of the streets, he is sure to be no less forcibly moved by the very different character of those parts which are termed 'the Liberties.' Here, narrow streets, houses without windows or doors, and several families crowded together beneath the same roof, present a picture of ruin, disease, poverty, filth, and wretchedness, of which they who have not witnessed it are unable to form a competent idea. Dublin, I have said, is a city of lamentable contrasts: so is London; but the contrasts of Dublin are brought more immediately together than those of the English metropolis. When Dublin presents a scene of the most enlivening gaiety, numbers of miserable beings may be seen lying half naked, and apparently half dead from cold and hunger, on the parapets and the steps of the houses, their nightly resting places; and the stranger, as he enters the hospitable abode which invites him to partake of the enjoyments and luxuries of life, is almost invariably saluted with the feeble cries and imploring accents of the wretched and the destitute.

The people of the Liberties, originally the area located outside the old city walls and so named because it was subject to private jurisdiction, lived in narrow streets along side slaughter houses, soap manufactories, carrion-houses and lime kilns. Thomas Cromwell, who visited the Liberties in 1820 commented:

> The streets in this quarter are mostly narrow; the lanes and alleys numerous; and the far greater number of houses, which are which are excessively crowded together, occupied by small tradesmen, artisans, the working poor, and beggars; from thirty to fifty, selected from which classes, are often resident in the same habitation; and the accumulation of filth, stench, and every variety of wretchedness resulting from this union of obnoxious circumstances, as well as from some peculiarly offensive habits in the people, is scarcely conceivable. Two, three, and even four families, consisting of persons of all ages and sexes, are known to club together as joint-tenants, for the purpose of defraying the rent of a single apartment in one of these distressful styles.

The closure of the Irish Parliament resulted in a mass exit of the gentry leaving for London, and the inner city became increasingly associated with poverty and slums as the population grew from 182,000 in 1800 to 285,000 in 1851.

The wealthy had vacated substantial townhouses in aristocratic districts such as Gardiner Street and Summer Hill on the Northside and these one-family homes were rapidly subdivided to accommodate at least one family per room. Diseases such as cholera, typhus and smallpox were endemic. Once generated, disease spread from room to room and from floor to floor of the city's slums and was carried back to the houses of the rich by servants and employees. Inadequate sewerage systems, poor water supplies, slaughter-houses, and obnoxious activities such as soap-making and lime-burning right in the midst of the crowded population all contributed to the situation.

By the end of the nineteenth century, the high mortality rate among the Dublin poor reached the outrageous figure of 33.6 per 1000; the London average was 19.6. The high rate was due largely to tuberculosis. Free disinfection was offered to the residents of any Dublin dwelling in which a person suffering from consumption had died, but in the majority of cases this offer was refused. One doctor complained, ' they will attend wakes, sleep, dwell or visit, in places teeming with infection, without a moment's misgiving, but as soon as ever the officer has been brought to disinfect a house or room, they shun it as if he had brought the plague instead of banishing it'.

Progress was made by Dublin Corporation over the years. More than 2,000 people in the Liberties were rehoused in the 1890s. Sanitary officers vigorously pursued, fined and named those found guilty of trading in adulterated food, and flush toilets spread rapidly after 1880. The Corporation took steps to close down dangerous housing, remove refuse, control slaughterhouses and appoint health inspectors. The migration of Dublin's wealthier households to the suburbs held back the city's capacity to address public health and housing issues until the beginning of the twentieth century, and it was not until the 1940s that a much delayed public-housing programme finally banished the slums.

The most backward towns in Ireland were generally in the interior where there were no flourishing industries to promote their growth. They were mere centres of exchange with the surrounding countryside where farmers and graziers came to dispose of their produce and to buy such commodities as they did not manufacture themselves. On market days and fair days these towns came to life. According to the *Statistical Survey of Armagh*, published in 1804:

> The fairs and markets are, in general, well attended by retailers of hats, stockings, shoes, cloth, and wool, from other counties; and also by pedlars, whose stock consists of articles of apparel, principally of women's wear, and hardware. These itinerant dealers are always travelling from one market town to another; some of them have no fixed residence.

Armagh market place in 1810. (Armagh Museum)

Going to market. (Richard Lovett, *Irish Pictures Drawn with Pen and Pencil*, 1888)

Author William Makepeace Thackeray described a fair he encountered at Nass in the 1840s:

> the town, as we drove into it, was thronged with frieze-coats, the market-place bright with a great number of apple-stalls, and the street filled with carts and vans of numerous small tradesmen, vending cheeses, or cheap crockeries, or ready-made clothes and such goods. A clothier, with a great crowd round him, had arrayed himself in a staring new waistcoat of his stock, and was turning slowly round to exhibit the garment, spouting all the while to his audience, and informing them that he could fit out any person, in one minute, 'in a complete new suit from head to fut'. There seemed to be a crowd of gossips at every shop-door, and, of course, a number of gentlemen waiting at the inn-steps, criticising the cars and carriages as they drove up.

The county frequently came to town in search of work, as American visitor Asenath Nicholson observed in the mid-1840s when visiting Galway:

> On my return to my lodgings, I saw a company of men assembled in a square, and found it was a collection of poor countrymen from distant parts, who had come hoping on the morrow to find a little work. Each man had his spade, and all were standing in a waiting posture, in silence, hungry and weary; for many had walked fifteen or twenty miles without eating, nor did they expect to eat that day. Sixpence a day was all they could get, and they could not afford food on the Sabbath, when they could not work. The countenance of one near me was a finished picture of despair, which said clearly, ' It is done: I can do no more.'

Fair day at Mountmellick, Laois.

Her landlord later told her that every week the poor come from the surrounding country and often stayed two days without eating, 'watching and hoping a chance may come; and sleep where they can; and then most of them go away, without getting any work.'

Many towns were small and almost invariably shabby, their approaches lined with poor hovels, their streets interspersed with ruins. Richard Coulter commented in 1862:

> Tuam is remarkable for the extent of its suburbs, which are larger in proportion than those of any other place that I have visited; and I regret to say that much poverty exists among the people who inhabit them. Rows of mud cabins extend in various directions, some to a distance of fully one mile from the town, and the aspect which they represent is miserable in the extreme.

Hardship in the surrounding countryside could have a major impact on the market towns as noted by Sir Francis Head in his *Fortnight in Ireland*, published in 1852. He asked the waiter at his hotel in Westport what impact recent evictions had had locally, 'They have ruined it,' he replied, 'the poor used to support the rich; now that the poor are gone the rich shopkeepers are all failing. Our town is full of empty shops, and, after all, the landlord himself is now being ruined!'

Until the mid-nineteenth century, a military barracks was often the only substantial building in the town. Shortly after the Union, it was estimated that there were between 30,000 and 50,000 regular troops stationed in Ireland,

The Square, Warrenpoint.

Belfast and Northern Counties railway terminus, York Road, Belfast, *c.* 1902.
(NLI Lawrence Royal 2430)

besides 21,000 militiamen and numerous bodies of yeomanry, so it is not surprising to find that military barracks were often the finest and most magnificent
buildings in the Irish towns of the period. The fact that town rents were often
higher in Ireland than in England was popularly ascribed to the temporary
residence of the military, and this probably helped to make them unpopular
with the inhabitants, especially as their behaviour was often far from orderly.
The soldiers were, however, often the chief support of the local tradesmen, the
officers generally dinning at taverns, while the common soldiers bought meat
and other provisions in the shops.

By the beginning of the Victorian era many of these towns included a
bank, and within twenty years, a railway station which carried agricultural
produce to the major ports. They were also important centres of administration with court houses, hospitals, workhouses and later council headquarters.
By the mid-nineteenth century, Irish towns were lit by gas as noted by Kohl
on his journey between Newry and Belfast in the 1840s, 'Nearly all the little
towns through which we passed that evening were lighted with gas. It is
remarkable how this important new invention has already penetrated all
through this country'. In his book *Ireland in 1839 and 1869*, H.S. Thompson
noted with approval:

> The evidences of increasing wealth are, however, by no means confined
> to the sea coast, or to private residences. In all the principal towns public
> buildings of a substantial and handsome appearance have been erected since

1839. New churches, banks, asylums, are everywhere to be met with, and English magistrates and guardians of the poor might with advantage visit the Irish court-houses and union workhouses. The ornamental character of these buildings is doubtless partly due to the beauty of the blue limestone of which they are for the most part built, but their designs show good taste, as well as fitness for their purpose, and the sites have in general been selected with great judgment, so that they contrast very favourably with the barrack-like appearance of the buildings in England.

Although visitors noted with approval many of the public buildings which adorned many towns, those streets that radiated off the main street were generally shabby. Coulter observed:

> The mass – I may say the whole of the cottages constituting the extensive suburbs of Tuam – are neither water-tight nor air-tight, and are unfit for the habitation of human beings, more especially in a season of severity like the present. The back lanes and streets without the town are occupied by artisans and labourers of the poorest class; the houses are of the most inferior description, and in many of them two or three families are congregated together, where they 'suffer in foulest rags each dire disease', and drain the bitter cup of poverty to its dregs.

Clogheen Main Street.

Killala. (Richard Lovett, *Irish Pictures Drawn with Pen and Pencil*, 1888)

This sort of deprivation was immeasurably worse in the great cities like Dublin and Belfast. Infectious diseases such as cholera, typhus and smallpox which periodically swept through the cities were directly related to the close and dirty living conditions of the slums. Once generated, disease spread uncontrollably from room to room and from floor to floor. The distant rich were not immune, as disease was carried back from the tenements through the visits of servants to their families. When disease arrived it was greeted with panic as noted by the *Galway Advertiser* for 14 July 1832:

> The inhabitants of Loughrea were completely panic struck on the first appearance of Cholera amongst them, so much so, that were it not for the great exertions of the above very active and efficient magistrate [James Hardiman Burke], the dead would have remained unburied. He was to be seen every place, without showing the least temerity or dread, by his presence, to allay fear, and by the weight of his influence, keep down any disposition to riot or confusion, as some of the patients' friends evinced a parallel inclina-

tion to their removal to Hospital. Not satisfied even with this, he dispatched his own car and horse to Galway, and brought a sufficient number of men to Loughrea to perform the office of interment.

To many visitors, Irish streets seemed to team with livestock or dangerous animals. Revd James Hall complained in 1812, 'there are acts of Parliament against pigs running in the streets, yet this act is daily and hourly broken in Cork, where pigs are sometimes so numerous, that you are not only often impeded in your walking by them, but sometimes likely to be overturned.' Dogs were also a nuisance, and considerably more dangerous to the public if the following notice from the *Cork Examiner* for 1 July 1863 is to be believed:

CAUTION TO THE OWNERS OF DOGS.
At the Police-office, yesterday morning, Mr. W. Johnson, the presiding magistrate, complained of the number of dogs without log or muzzle now straying about the city. He said that a person could not go into one of the back streets of the city without being followed by troops of snarling curs, who were not only most annoying, but were also most dangerous, several persons having been lately bit. He then directed the Police throughout the city to summons the owners of those dogs, and promised if they were brought before him to inflict the full penalty of 10s. and costs.

The Mall, Waterford.

The Quays, Waterford.

More extensive towns and cities were to be found on the coast, but even here visitors paint a picture of poverty and decline. Worse still, many visitors to Irish towns were unimpressed by the social life. In *Three Months in Ireland*, Madame de Bovet declared, 'As in most Irish towns, the capital included, life for the inhabitants of Waterford is dull enough – no aristocracy, no upper middle class, little money, the horizon bounded by local politics. The county, of which it is the principal town, possesses no fewer than eleven newspapers.'

Lying south of the great grazing counties, Cork became an important city during the eighteenth century, exporting large quantities of provisions to the Continent, to the English colonies in America, and to the West Indies. The trade of Cork, with its population of about 80,000 inhabitants, had grown so great by the end of the eighteenth century that it was known as the 'Bristol of Ireland'. By the nineteenth century, however, it was a town in decline. Dr John Forbes, during a visit in the early 1850s, found similar conditions of wealth and poverty which he had encountered in Dublin:

> Like all large towns, and more especially the large towns of Ireland, Cork contains masses of hidden streets of the most squalid description, inhab-
> ited by a ragged and seemingly wretched population. In passing through
> such streets, however, it is but just to the inhabitants to state that we
> saw no riotous or indecorous behaviour, and were but rarely solicited for
> charity. In going along the better streets, on Sunday, we observed many
> wretched-looking women, most of them with ragged children on their

St Patrick's Bridge, Cork.

laps or by their side, squatted in the recesses of the doors of the shut
shops, obviously beggars, yet not begging, except with that speaking look
of misery more emphatic than words. Even the children were as silent as
their mothers.

Limerick carried on a good trade in corn and provisions, for although the
city was more than sixty miles from the sea, ships of 500 tons were able to
sail up the Shannon and unload their cargoes at the quays. Walking through
the district of Newtown Pery in the 1840s William Makepeace Thackeray
commented:

> you are at first led to believe that you are arrived in a second Liverpool, so
> tall are the warehouses and broad the quays; so neat and trim a street of near
> a mile which stretches before you. But even this mile-long street does not,
> in a few minutes, appear to be so wealthy and prosperous as it shows at first
> glance; for of the population that throng the streets, two-fifths are barefooted
> women, and two-fifths more ragged men: and the most part of the shops
> which have a grand show with them appear, when looked into, to be no
> better than they should be, being empty makeshift-looking places with their
> best goods outside.

Henry Inglis, visiting Limerick a few years before Thackeray, was struck by the
inequalities between the good and bad quarters of the town:

Thomond Bridge, Limerick. (*Atlas and Cyclopedia of Ireland*, 1900)

A person arriving in Limerick by one of the best approaches, and driving to an hotel in George Street, will probably say, 'What a very handsome city this is!' while, on the other hand, a person entering the city by the old town, and taking up his quarters there – a thing, indeed, not likely to happen – would infallibly set down Limerick as the very vilest town he had ever entered.

Of the new town he commented:

The new town of Limerick is, unquestionably, superior to any thing out of Dublin. Its principal street, although less picturesque than the chief streets of Cork, would generally be reckoned a finer street. Its is straight, regular, and modern-looking; and contains abundance of good private houses and of excellent shops: and although there is less the appearance of business in Limerick than in Cork, and fewer evidences of affluence in its neighbour-hood; yet, in the more modern aspect of every thing, there are more certain proofs of improvement than in the former city.

Agriculture was the basis of Galway's economy during the eighteenth century with numerous mills for grain, oatmeal and malt. The arrival of the Midland Great Western Railway, which opened its line for traffic from Dublin to Galway on 1 August 1851, had a major impact on the city, boosting the tourist traffic to the west and providing the means of escape for thousands of emigrants who left the city in search of employment or a new future. However, nineteenth-century visitors describe it as a place in decline. According to Alexander Innes Shand who visited Galway in 1884:

The decay of a once prosperous town has more than kept pace with the diminishing of the sea traffic. Except for the signs of age that make ruin seem respectable, a walk about the principal streets leaves the impression of a city sacked and bombarded. Galway looks like Strasburg as I saw it immediately after Strasburg's capture by the Germans. There are roofless houses without end; there are abandoned tenements with shivered window-panes, or else with the doors and windows boarded up. Aristocratic mansions, with coats of arms and bishops' mitres on their sculptured facades, have been degraded into whisky shops and mean grocery stores. As for those great warehouses near the wharves, they are spectral in their desolation.

Irish towns and cities received an unwelcome impetus from the Great Famine as many sought refuge in the workhouses, in hospitals and various charitable institutions. On 25 February 1847, the editor of the *Newry Telegraph* drew attention to the fact that the soup kitchen which had been established in Newry was encouraging the destitute poor from the outlying regions to come into the town:

For weeks past, there have been observable in our streets numbers of mendicants with whose faces frequency of their appearance had not rendered the community familiar … they travel into the town in quest of food, not obtainable in their own localities. Squalid objects they generally are. Their appearance sufficiently attests that their plea of want is no deceptive subterfuge. In nine cases out of every ten, moreover, in reply to your questioning, you have from these evidently distressed supplicants for alms the statement, that they had patiently endured privations rather than beg, but that, disease having been superinduced by insufficiency of the necessaries of life, and innutritiousness of the food scantily partaken of, they had had no alternative but either to allow sufferers from "the complaint" to perish of hunger or come into Newry and seek for bread, no relief being obtainable in their part of the country.

The influx of these starving and destitute multitudes into the towns and cities excited more than pity. There was the fear of fever which provoked even greater inhumanity in the fearful townsfolk. John East who witnessed this phenomenon in Cork commented:

Now and then might be seen a number of persons running to a particular spot; and, on inquiry, you would hear of one having sunk to the earth in the sudden crisis of fever, or in death itself. From ten to fifteen bodies would be found in the streets, at the dawn of every returning day. A labouring man told his clergyman, that, in going direct from his own door to his work, he saw, in a single morning, five corpses in the way. So great was the alarm of fever, that numbers were daily expelled from the low lodging-houses into the streets, as soon as the malady appeared. I myself saw and conversed with a family, consisting of a mother and three children, who had been discarded from a brother's house; and all their shelter in cold, stormy, and drenching weather, was a broken dresser, placed against a wall, in a vacant space, between two houses. There lay a boy in fever; while his mother and two sisters were sitting on the ground beside him!

The Great Famine, which devastated much of the Ulster countryside, contributed to the rapid expansion of many towns across Ireland but nowhere more so than Belfast, as people fled to the town in hope of work or charity. During the second half of the nineteenth century Belfast grew more rapidly than any other city in the British Isles, with its population increasing from 22,000 in 1806 to nearly 340,000 ninety years later.

During the first thirty years of the nineteenth century the cotton and linen industries helped transform Belfast from a small town into a major industrial

Child poverty in Belfast, early 1900s. (Ulster Museum)

city. The confidence of the Belfast middle classes by the beginning of the nine-teenth century was expressed by the *Belfast Almanack* for 1803. 'This Town', it boasted 'for extent, population, commerce, and manufactures, is justly consid-ered as the capital of the north of Ireland'. It was the integrity of its merchant class which had brought about this happy state of affairs:

> The inhabitants, by their industry and spirit of enterprise, have extended their commerce to almost every part of the trading world, except where exclusive privileges, to chartered bodies, mark the bounds of their extension. The general character of its merchants has not a little contributed to its pros-perity; for *punctuality, integrity* and *strict honour* in their commercial pursuits, they have always stood highly conspicuous. *These* pillars of commerce have been the support of its merchants through their progressive state, and laid the foundation of their present extended credit, consequence and wealth.

By the middle of the nineteenth century, Belfast with its thirty-two linen mills with over half a million spindles, was well on its way to replacing Leeds and Dundee as the major linen manufacturer in the country. Mr and Mrs Hall were impressed by the industrial character of the city which set it apart from the others they had visited in Ireland.

> It is something new to perceive rising above the houses numerous tall and thin chimneys which are indicative of industry, occupation, commerce and prosperity, with the volumes of smoke that issued from them giving unques-tionable tokens of full employment, while its vicinity to the ocean removed at once all idea that the labour was unwholesome or the labourers unhealthy.

They went on to declare that, 'The clean and bustling appearance of Belfast is decidedly unnational. That it is in Ireland, but not of it, is a remark often on the lips of visitors from the south or west.'

The rapid growth of Belfast had a profound impact on the people who arrived in the town from the surrounding countryside as noted by the author of *Ireland Picturesque and Romantic* (1838). Leitch Ritchie visited the town at the very beginning of the Victorian age and was impressed by what he saw:

> The streets, generally speaking, are wide and well aired, and the houses by which they are lined, clean and respectable, although built of unstuc-coed brick as plain as a bandbox. The suburbs, inhabited by the hewers of wood and drawers of water to the easier classes, having nothing of that filth and misery which are almost an unfailing characteristic of an Irish town.

Everything in and around Belfast proclaims that it is the abiding place of a shrewd and intelligent population devoted to worldly gain and far from being unsuccessful in its pursuits. This of course is a general picture; for a town which has more than doubled its numbers three times within the last seventy years must draw constant supplies from the country; and to correct the habitual imprudence and want of neatness observable in the Irish peasant must be a work of time. A considerable number of the masters, however, now provide their workmen with lodgings; and some of these establishments are clean and wholesome, and extremely neat ...

William Makepeace Thackeray, soon to be famous as the author of *Vanity Fair*, visited Belfast during the early 1840s. He was especially impressed by the bustling nature of the northern town:

They call Belfast the Irish Liverpool; if people are for calling names, it would be better to call it the Irish London at once – the chief city of the kingdom, at any rate. It looks hearty, thriving, and prosperous, as if it had money in its pockets, and roast-beef for dinner: it has no pretensions to fashion, but looks, mayhap better in its honest broadcloth than *some people* in their shabby brocade.

Belfast Lough. (W.H. Bartlett, *The Scenery and Antiquities of Ireland*, 1841)

In common with other industrial cities of the time, Belfast had its share of slum
housing in which the poor were forced to live in the most desperate conditions. Periodic slumps in the textile or cotton industries left many unemployed
and forced to depend on charity. Those in work were often on the breadline
when hard seasons raised the price of food. With widespread destitution came
diseases such as cholera and typhus. According to the Revd W.H. O'Hanlon,
Congregationalist minister for Upper Donegall Street church in the city, writing in the 1850s:

> plunging into the alleys and entries of this neighbourhood, what indescrib-
> able scenes of poverty, filth, and wretchedness everywhere meet the eye!
> Barrack-lane was surely built when it was imagined the world would soon
> prove too strait for the number of its inhabitants. About five or six feet is the
> space here allotted for the passage of the dwellers, and for the pure breath of
> heaven to find access to their miserable abodes. But, in truth, no pure breath
> of heaven ever enters here; it is tainted and loaded by the most noisome,
> reeking feculence, as it struggles to reach these loathsome hovels. These are,
> in general, tenanted by two families in each, and truly it is a marvel and a
> mystery how human beings can, in such a position, escape disease in its
> most aggravated and pestilential forms. I know not whether it would ser-
> vice any valuable purpose to reveal the names of the proprietors of such
> horrid homesteads. But, surely, they must be comparatively ignorant of the
> sanitary condition of the tenements from which their agents extract their
> weekly rents. That property has its duties as well as its rights, is a sentiment
> not less applicable on a small scale than upon one of the wildest dimensions;
> but the principle seems to be lost sight of in such squalid rotten nooks as
> the one now described.

As in the country, the loss of a breadwinner could spell disaster for the urban
poor as Revd O'Hanlon observed, 'In M'Tier's-court we found fever doing its
work; the husband of a poor woman had just gone to the hospital, leaving her,
meanwhile, to starve or beg, or what seems to such persons, for some reason or
other, the worse of all expedients, to knock on the poorhouse gate.' O'Hanlon
thought that the country dweller:

> without any romance or sickly sentimentalism, is it not a mighty advantage he
> possesses over the suffocated artisan, and others still lower down in the social
> scale, in our densely crowded cities? I may be met by figures and statistics, but
> however dry, very dry, and hard and cold these may be, I cannot for the life
> of me be made to think, that Samuel-street and its environs, that Grey's-lane,

the common surface sewer of the whole region, that Peel's court, with its twelve families in six houses, and shut in – narrow and close – between two nuisance-yards, one for the front and another for the back, where the air is such that we could not stand a moment, without a sense of deadly sickness and loathing warning us to flee from the foul spot – I cannot, Sir, persuade myself, with all the aid of learned statisticians, that these places can supply any advantages of a city life to counterbalance the noisome and noxious evils which they engender and diffuse.

The rapid industrial growth of Belfast also brought other problems. As Belfast's population grew, clashes between the different religious groups became an increasing feature of life in the town. Sectarian rivalry manifested itself in waves of rioting beginning with a clash on 12 July 1813 and continuing through-out the nineteenth and twentieth centuries. Polling day battles in 1832, 1835 and 1841 had become by 1857 serious rioting that lasted for days or weeks. Various constitutional crises during the nineteenth century only exasperated sectarianism within Belfast. As the south and west of the country pressed for a parliament in Dublin, Belfast's strongly Protestant and Unionist majority made preparations to resist Irish Home Rule by force. Sir Edward Cowan reminded his counterparts in Dublin that Belfast, with a large proportion of the popula-tion and so much of the wealth, would have a say about the future and that such 'a large town, backed by so large a part of the province, forms and must form an important factor, which will have to be taken into consideration by those who call out for Home Rule, Nationalism, and Ireland for the Irish'. By 1912, Belfast had become the centre of opposition to Home Rule for Ireland, and within a year an army, the Ulster Volunteer Force, had been formed to underline its determination to resist its imposition at all costs. More than a century of religious conflict was about to begin.

4

WORKING LIFE

The Industrial Revolution did not have the same dramatic impact in Ireland as it did in Britain during the late eighteenth century. But Ireland's proximity to Britain, then the greatest industrial nation in the world, had a dramatic impact on its fragile economy. Mass-produced British goods were so much cheaper than the corresponding Irish goods, and the improved transportation systems within

Drogheda Railway Bridge under construction. (Richard Lovett, 1888)

The launch of the SS *Aurora*, 1824. (Mary Lowry, *The Story of Belfast*, 1913)

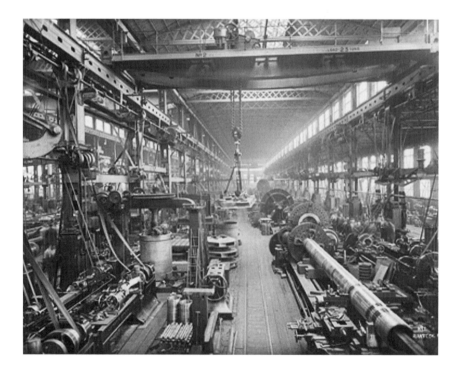

Turning shop engineering department, Harland and Wolff, 1897. (Ulster Museum)

Ireland with the development of the canals and later the coming of the railways, served to open up the Irish market to its competitors. The only exception was the north-east where heavy investment in industrial processes improved the productivity of the linen, cotton and shipbuilding industries making many of its firms, such as Harland and Wolff, world famous.

For most of its history Ireland has been a largely agricultural economy and the great landowners were an important source of employment. Right up until the First World War and in some cases beyond this period, servants were an integral part of big-house life in Ireland. They ensured a luxurious and leisured lifestyle for landlords by taking care of everything from caring for the richly furnished interiors of houses to cultivating extensive and elaborate gardens. The larger the house, the larger the number of servants required to cope with the number of tasks involved. Recruitment of staff was usually through personal recommendations, particularly at the higher levels of housekeeper, governess and cook. Local Irish women found most opportunities for employment at the lower levels as maids in the house, kitchen, nursery or dairy.

According to the 1871 census, domestic service accounted for almost 15 per cent of the female workforce. Servant life was not an easy one. Staff could be dismissed for unsatisfactory service. Mr and Mrs Hall condemned the treatment of Irish servants, 'They are insufficiently remunerated; little care is bestowed upon their wants; they are seldom properly fed and lodged …' An 'odious and evil custom' which they took objection to was the mode of paying servants what was called 'breakfast money' which was a small allowance allotted to them by their employees for food and the other necessities of life:

> The almost inevitable consequence is that of the weekly allowance they contrive to save a considerable portion, or nearly the whole, usually with a view to devoting the quarter's wages untouched to the necessities of their more miserable families 'at home'… thus they are subjected to severe privations in the midst of plenty, if they scrupulously abstain from taking that which, by this rule, is not to belong to them.

Mary MacMahon agreed. In 1857, she complained:

> The servant on a miserable pittance is expected to have the virtues of a seraph and the capacity for drudgery of a slave. She must not think of dress, of news, of acquaintance, or of pleasure of any kind … It is impossible for them to make provision for old age or sickness, and yet in many families there is no kindly consideration shown for them. Many a lady that drives in her carriage and sports needless finery on her person, is overbearing, and penurious to her servants.

Certain families provided servants over several generations in the same house. More considerate estate owners provided a small pension or lodgings on the estate for long-term employees. By that time such servants were almost part of the family, and on the sort of familiar terms that surprised visitors. Kohl found on his travels in Ireland in the mid-1840s:

> In England, where servants are kept at a proper distance, it is seldom that they venture on the familiar impertinence of which I saw frequent instances in Ireland. My worthy friend's coachman, a well-fed, merry-looking fellow, accompanied us through the stables and farm buildings, and pointed out every remarkable object to my attention, with a constant flow of eloquence, while his master followed modestly behind us. 'This stable you see, sir,' proceeded the coachman, 'we finished last year. And a deal of trouble it cost us, for we had to begin by blowing away the whole of the rock there. But we shall have a beautiful prospect for our pains when the trees yonder have been cut down. And look down there, your honour, all them is his dominions (pointing to his master), and in two months he'll have finished the new building he has begun.' Now no English servant would have made equally free with his master, and yet the Irish servants are taken from a far more dependant class than the English peasants.

Until the First World War most big houses imported their upper servants from England, Scotland or Northern Ireland, usually reliably Protestant. This sometimes led to tension below stairs with the Irish Catholic servants who were suspect as 'disloyal'. A glance at the Wanted section of Victorian newspapers confirms this. On 17 January 1860 the following advertisement appeared in *The Irish Times*:

> WANTED – COUNTY LIMERICK – A BUTLER, where a footman is kept; Protestant, and of best character and ability. Also as LODGE KEEPER, man and wife (with no young children), pensioner, soldier, or policeman. The man, if handy, could get daily employment about the farm. Protestants preferred.

Another important source of employment in the countryside was spinning and weaving, in which women and children played an important role in bringing in extra money to the household. Wool spinning was concentrated in the southern part of Ireland, in Counties Cork, Kilkenny and Tipperary. Although the 1841 Census recorded that over 70,000 women were engaged in spinning wool, many of the 300,000 unspecified spinners may also have done so.

In many parts of Connaught and north Leinster a woman's income from spinning was more regular than a man's earnings from agricultural labour, and
women often provided the main cash income for a household. Spinning was
mechanised during the late eighteenth century, long before weaving, but the
workers' skills were soon in demand in the new cotton mills where women
and children formed most of the workforce.

Weaving was also a major source of employment, particularly amongst
men, until the early twentieth century, in both the towns and the countryside.
Weaving did not become mechanised as quickly as spinning but the change
was taking place in the 1840s as Kohl noted on his travels through Ireland:

> A very considerable quantity of the linen, I believe much more than one-
> half, is still made in the country by hand-looms; yet 'power-weaving' as the
> English call weaving by machinery, is increasing every day. The melancholy
> and much-felt battle between the hand-loom and the power-loom, which in
> some towns of England has been decided in favour of the latter, is going on
> in Belfast.

During periods of depression in the linen industry, weavers could be hit
very hard. On a visit to Ballymena and the Galgorm Estate, Margaret Dixon
McDougall commented:

> It is in the country parts, more remote from the public eye, that one sees
> the destitution wrought by the depression in the linen trade. People there
> are struggling with all their might to live and keep out of the workhouses.
> Hand-loom weaving seems doomed to follow hand-spinning and become a
> thing of the past. Weavers some time ago had a plot of ground which brought
> potatoes and kale to supplement the loom, and on it could earn twelve shil-
> lings a week. But alas! while the webs grew longer the price grew less and
> they are in a sad case.

She called at the home of one weaver and described him as 'an intelligent man,
with the prevailing Scotch type of face' and found him:

> accompanied by a sickly wife, sitting by a scanty fire, ragged enough. This
> man for his last web was paid at the rate of twopence a yard for weaving linen
> with twenty hundred threads to the inch, but out of this money he had to
> buy dressing and light, and have some one, the sickly wife I suppose, to wind
> the bobbins for him. He must then pay rent for the poor cabin he lived in,
> none too good for a stable, and supply all his wants on the remainder.

Linen Hall, Belfast. (Richard Lovett, *Irish Pictures Drawn with Pen and Pencil*, 1888)

The weavers she met blamed the concentration of the trade in the hands of a few manufacturers for the reduction in wages. They were obliged to take the yarn from a manufacturer and return it to him in cloth, whereas before they could sell it for the best price. Their poverty was compounded by the fact that they had no garden in which to grow potatoes and so had nothing to fall back on when wages were low. Margaret Dixon McDougall found that such views found little favour with their wealthier neighbours; 'the large majority blame the improvidence of the poor.' They eat bacon and drink tea where potatoes and milk or porridge and milk used to be good enough for them.' She added drily: 'It is difficult to imagine the extravagance.'

At such times many fled to the towns in search of work. This led to a great deal of bitterness, as labourers in the countryside were usually prepared to work for lower wages than their town counterparts, a situation that employers were only to happy to exploit. In the towns, skilled tradesmen could command fairly high wages and they were not slow to take advantage of their position. Gerald Fitzgibbon wrote in 1868:

> The only complaints I have heard in respect of these skilled tradesmen and town labourers, have come from their employers; and the substance of these complaints has been, that the workmen, finding the wages of three, four, or five days of the week sufficient to supply their wants, and to gratify their appetites, they idle for one, two, or three days, to the great injury and inconvenience of their masters, and that the competition for them is so great, that the employers find it difficult to govern their men; and are obliged to connive and be silent at misconduct, which would not be ensured under a different state of things.

In Dublin, skilled workers belonged to guilds which controlled the conditions of work and the entry into a trade through apprenticeships. There were also mutual protection societies which provided for the poor, sick and needy. Dublin had twenty-five trade guilds: some, such as those of the bakers, the glovers and skinners and the shoemakers or cordwainers dated from the fifteenth century while others, including the carpenters, millers, masons, goldsmiths and clockmakers received their charters in Tudor times. Catholics were not formally admitted until 1793 but quickly exerted their influence as several of the guilds actually declared for Catholic Emancipation by the 1820s.

These guilds declined after the Union with the formation of combinations (early unions) among the unskilled workmen, who were not afraid to use violence to secure their demands. Those who refused to join them were often in danger of their lives. A master-shipbuilder told the Government Commission in 1836:

> Ireland is the dearest country in the world for labour every description of artisan demands at least one-third more than in England; there is even a combination among the common porters in the quarry, who would rather starve than work under the regulated price … I am so disgusted at the conduct of the men [he adds] that I am resolved never to drive another nail here, if I can possibly avoid it.

These combinations raised wage levels to such an extent in Dublin that they undermined the trades to which they belonged. A Mr Otway told the Hand Loom Weaver Commission that:

> It cannot be doubted that illegal and dangerous combinations among the workmen have operated most injuriously on the trade, driven many of the most extensive manufacturers out of it, and deterred others from directing

that capital and intelligence towards it by which alone it be preserved or enabled to compete with the other silk-weaving districts of the Empire. If not checked, this system will speedily drive away the portion of the silk trade which now remains.

Many of the better silk weavers fled to Manchester and other silk-weaving districts in England owing to the tyranny of these combinations.

It is certainly true that nineteenth-century Dublin did not enjoy the sort of industrial boom which various towns and cities in the north of England enjoyed. The chief industrial wealth of Dublin in the eighteenth century came from woollen manufacture. It had expanded rapidly with the opening of direct trade with North America, the main source of raw materials, and with the encouragement given by the Irish Parliament. By the beginning of the nineteenth century however, the 300 looms still working in Dublin could not compete with the new English power looms and the industry in the south went into rapid decline.

In the north, cotton manufacture remained strong with employers enjoying the double advantage of sufficient capital to buy machinery and the proximity of cheap coal from Lancashire. John Milford's mill in Winetavern Street was five storeys high and its 5,364 spindles and 24 carding machines were turned by a ten-horsepower engine. In 1811 the Revd Dubourdieu calculated that in the Belfast area there were 150,000 power-driven spindles making over 70 million hanks of cotton yard, and concluded 'that not less then 30,000 individuals derive a good support from the muslin and calico branches of this trade, taking in all the different departments'. The factories spun cotton by steam or water power; this mill yarn was then 'put out' to hand-loom weavers to be made into cloth. They could be fined for any flaws or for days overdue. They were in no position to object because they had become dependent on the mill owners for their livelihood.

Already the cotton industry in the north was being eclipsed by the newly mechanised linen mills. Belfast stood at the heart of the linen industry. John Barrow, who visited the town in the mid-1830s was struck by the:

verdant fields, intersected by bleaching-grounds covered with linen as white as snow – afforded a cheerful and lively prospect, more particularly to a stranger not accustomed in his own country to look upon the latter object. The linen is laid out in long strips, the width of the web, and, with the blades of grass standing up between them, has the effect, from a little distance, which is produced just when the snow is in the act of dissolving with the warmth of the sun.

In 1850, a third of the flax-spinning mills, producing over half of the linen output for all of Ireland, were located in the Belfast area. In 1830 there were two linen mills in Belfast; by 1850 there were thirty-two with over half a million spindles. William Makepeace Thackeray wrote in 1840, 'A fine night-exhibition in the town is that of the huge spinning-mills which surround it, and of which the thousand windows are lighted up at nightfall, and may be seen from almost all quarters of the city.' Thackeray visited Mulholland's five-storey factory in York Street. Originally a cotton factory, it had burned down in 1828. It was replaced by a five-storey factory with three steam engines driving some 8,000 flax-spinning spindles. Thackeray was impressed by the scale of the operations:

> There are nearly 500 girls employed in it. They work in huge long chambers, lighted by numbers of windows, hot with steam, buzzing and humming with hundreds of thousands of whirling wheels, that all take their motion from a steam-engine which lives apart in a hot cast-iron temple of its own, from which it communicates with the innumerable machines that the five hundred girls preside over … They work for twelve hours daily, in rooms of which the heat is intolerable to a stranger; but in spite of it they looked gay, stout, and healthy; nor were their forms much concealed by the very simple clothes they wear while in the mill.

The spinning mills where built in green-field sites along the Lower Falls and Shankill Roads and formed the nucleus of West Belfast. The mill owners built row upon row of terraced houses for their rapidly expanding workforce. In these houses close-knit communities developed with each generation following its predecessor into the spinning mills and factories. These areas soon developed along sectarian lines as Catholic workers settled in the Falls Road area while Protestants gravitated towards the Shankill, Ballymacarrett and Ballynafeigh region.

Few attempts were made to ensure safer conditions in the mills and factories in Ireland until the twentieth century. Linen workers ran the risk of being maimed or killed by exposed machinery. Injury and death were endemic and frequent accounts of accidents appear in local newspapers. The *Belfast News Letter*, 1 May 1854, reported that an employee of Messrs Rowan of York Street had suffered terrible injuries and was not expected to recover, 'She was engaged at the carding part of the machinery and her hair by some means got entangled in the machinery in which the greater part of the scalp was removed from the head'. The *Belfast News Letter*, 24 May 1880, recounts the death that took place in the early hours of Saturday morning at the extensive establishment of Combe, Barbour and Combe, Falls Foundry, 'A man named John Keown, residing in Woodburn Street, whiles engaged at a steam crane in the moulding shop ... was caught in the crane, and received such injuries as to cause almost instantaneous death.' At the subsequent coroner's inquest, his workmates provided evidence of the accident.

> Patrick McAvoy ... saw the deceased's arm caught and the clothes torn off it by the shafting and gearing. McIntyre Sheals deposed to getting the engine stopped by the driver. George Robinson, superintendent engineer, said that the machinery in which the deceased was caught could not be stopped without the engine being stopped. He believed that even if the engine had been stopped almost immediately the man's life could not have been saved, as the shaft that he was caught in was going at the rate of 100 revolutions a minute.

The jury returned a verdict of accidental death, but recommended that the machinery in question be fenced to prevent such an accident in the future.

Some employers could be more enlightened in their dealings with employees, although, in one case at least, this ended in tragedy, according to the *Southern Patriot* of 28 February 1844::

> DREADFUL ACCIDENT.
> Some time ago a labouring man in the employment of the Messrs. Allen, millers, of Shannon Vale, about two miles from the town of Clonakilty, died, leaving a wife and family to deplore his loss. With a feeling of humanity which does them credit, the proprietors allowed his poor widow three shillings a week for her support, and she, to prove her gratitude for such extreme liberality, went to the mill every day, for the purpose of mending empty bags and keeping the place clean. One morning, about a week ago, as she was preparing for her accustomed labour, having gone too near the machinery, her clothes were caught by the cogs of one of the wheels, and before the slightest assistance could be given, she was crushed to death; her two legs being completely severed from the body, which was otherwise shockingly disfigured. The mill was stopped as soon as possible, and the unfortunate woman conveyed to her own house, where an inquest was held, and a verdict of accidental death returned. What adds to this melancholy affair is the fact that the deceased was far advanced in a state of pregnancy.

For those who survived the experience, conditions in the factories and mills were often primitive. In 1867 Dr John Moore, writing on the influence of flax-spinning on the health of mill workers, was concerned about the spinning rooms where, 'little girls are engaged, and here it is that the tender form of childhood is often in danger of being taxed beyond that it is able to bear'. Ten years later, Dr C.D. Purdon drew attention to the damaging effect of flax dust on the lungs of mill workers. He found that their 'mortality from Phthisis, etc., is very high ... this affection of the lungs, that flax dressers suffer so much from, is so well known to the army surgeons that they have forbidden the recruiting sergeants to enlist any from this department'. In the case of machine boys, Dr Purdon found that dust was so dense that it quickly entered the lungs. 'In severe and well marked attacks', he concluded, the paroxysm of cough and dyspnoea lasts for a considerable time, and does not pass off until the contents of the stomach are ejected, and often blood is spat up. He continued:

> In a great number of instances the lad is obliged to leave the mill, and seek for employment in healthier trades. But still in cold weather he suffers from cough and shortness of breath, and in many cases his life is terminated by Phthisis ... numbers linger out a diseased existence, in other callings, only to terminate in death.

Workers also suffered from exhaustion. Employers got around the 1847 Factory Act, limiting hours of work for women and children to ten a day, by introducing a relay system. According to Dr Moore:

> Those who have been long in the atmosphere of the spinning-room generally become pale and anaemic, and consequently pre-disposed to those ailments which spring from such a state of constitution. Children placed there early and compelled to keep upon their feet the entire day, as the nature of their employment obliges them to do often, suffer from the young and tender bones, which form the arch of the foot, being crushed and flattened.

It was not until 1874 that hours were successfully cut down to ten every weekday and six on Saturdays, and even then, employers added an extra duty of cleaning machines after hours. Until 1874 the usual working day began at 5 a.m. and ended at 7 or 8 p.m. Thereafter, until the beginning of the twentieth century, the working day began at 6.30 a.m. and finished at 6 p.m., with two three-quarter-hour breaks.

In 1835, the Herdman brothers, James, John and George from Belfast, decided to build a flax-spinning mill near to the flax fields of Donegal and the north-west of Ireland. Sion Mills, County Tyrone, was chosen as a rural area of high unemployment and with enormous waterpower. The Herdmans were determined to create a moral, God-fearing, temperate, educated, non-sectarian community around a flax-spinning business in the north-west of Ireland, which was a prolific flax-growing area. They built a model village, a school, churches, recreational and sporting facilities and succeededing in creating a community where everyone, of both religious, traditions lived together. The Halls, when they visited in 1840 found:

> Cottages, of simple construction, but sound and comfortable, have been built for the workmen and their families; a school is established, and to the Sunday school the Messrs. Herdman themselves attend, taking the greatest interest in the education progress of their work people, and distributing motives to improvement, lavishly and judicially …

Workers were drawn from the surrounding countryside. The Halls saw the Herdmans as beneficent employers rescuing their workforce, consisting of women and girls, from 'cowering over the embers of their turf fires, or begging along the waysides for morsels of food'. Factory life did not suit everyone, however, as noted by William Henry Hurlbert when staying at Sion House, County Tyrone, in the late 1880s:

Thomas Gallaher's tobacco factory, York Street, Belfast, *c.* 1900. (Ulster Museum)

After luncheon we walked with Mr. Herdman through the mills and the model village which has grown up around them. Everywhere we found order, neatness, and thrift. The operatives are almost all people of the country, Catholics and Protestants in almost equal numbers. 'I find it wise,' said Mr. Herdman, 'to give neither religion a preponderance, and to hold my people of both religions to a common standard of fidelity and efficiency.' The greatest difficulty he has had to contend with is the ineradicable objection of some of the peasantry to continuous industry. He told us of a strapping lass of eighteen who came to the mills, but very soon gave up and went back to the parental shebeen in the mountains rather than get up early in the morning to earn fourteen shillings a week.

With so many women and children employed in the factories, an increasing number of mill owners began to take a growing interest in their welfare. Dunbar, McMaster and Co. built the village of Dunbarton (named after Hugh Barton, its owner) near Gilford, County Down, where rows of terraced houses were built during the 1830s and 1840s by the company. Each house received a monthly inspection from the company, which also executed all repairs and maintenance free of charge. The company's willingness to take responsibility for its employees' lives even extended to the provision of schools, churches, shops and voluntary organisations.

Weaving factory. (Hogg Collection, Ulter Museum).

Many towns and villages would develop around the mill and factory. Milford, a few miles west of Armagh City, grew up around the McCrum weaving factory, while the village of Laurelvale was founded in the 1850s by Thomas Sinton to house the workers in his linen mill. Best known is the model village of Bessbrook, which was founded by John Pollock in 1759 but remodelled by Quaker John Grubb Richardson in 1845 with spacious squares surrounding the large linen mill owned by the family. Planned on the lines of a William Penn settlement, the village represented an experiment in

Joy's Paper Mill, Belfast, 1800. (Mary Lowry, *The Story of Belfast*, 1913)

social reform begun in 1845 by John Grubb Richardson. High quality houses were built, but it was the absence of a police station, public house or pawn shop which aroused the curiosity of visitors. George Bernard Shaw visited Bessbrook in 1879, commenting that, 'Bessbrook is a model village where the inhabitants never swear nor get drunk and look as if they would very much like to do both.'

Factories provided employment for entire families. At Gilford Margaret Dixon McDougall found:

> The wages of a common operative here is twelve shillings (or three dollars) per week. If they have a family grown up until they are able to work at the mills, of course it adds materially to the income. Girls are more precious than boys, I have heard, as being more docile and easier kept in clothing. They can earn about half wages, or six shillings (one dollar and a half) per week. Rents are about two shillings (or half a dollar) per week.

Families could suffer extreme hardship during slumps in the industry. Margaret Dixon McDougall commented while at Tandragee in the 1880s:

> Visited a great thread factory, where the yarn is made ready that is woven into double damask, and thread for all purposes supplied to all parts. In whatever part of Ireland the tall factory chimney rises up into the air the people have not the look of starvation that is stamped on the poor elsewhere. Still, if we consider a wage of seven to twelve shillings a week – twelve in this factory was the general wages – and subtract from that two shillings a week for the house and three shillings a week for fuel the operators are not likely to lay up large fortunes. As they have no gardens to the houses owned by the factory, nor backyard accommodation of any kind, the cleanliness and tidy appearance of houses and workpeople are a credit to them. But when times grow hard, and the mills run half time, and not even a potato to fall back upon, there must be great suffering behind these walls.

Most women in towns filled less skilled, poorly paid occupations. In the mid-1830s women in the Cork City parish of Shandon sorted feathers, prepared offal for market, and collected wash and grain from the city distillery to feed their pigs. Others sold old clothes, shoes, potatoes, vegetables and dairy products. In *An Account of Ireland, Statistical and Political*, published in 1812, Edward Wakefield complained that:

Women in Ireland are treated more like beasts of burden than rational beings, and although I never saw one yoked to a plough ... I have seen them degraded in a manner disgraceful to the other sex, and shocking to humanity. In the country they are subjected to all the drudgery generally performed by men; setting potatoes, digging turf, and the performance of the most laborious occupations. I have often watched them with the utmost attention, but never heard a woman disobey the command of her husband, or repine at his orders.

There were few areas of employment which middle-class women could enter. Teaching and governessing were two of the mainstays for those forced to support themselves. Shop work was also considered respectable work for young women. Shop assistants worked long hours, six days a week. Wages were not much better than that of factory workers, though shop assistants had to maintain a higher standard in appearance and dress. Office work also began to open up for women at the turn of the century. Women within offices had lower status than men and also became associated with the less well-paid areas of typing and book-keeping. The expanding public sector also opened up clerical opportunities for women. The Post Office was regarded as the pioneer of women's employment, offering positions as telegraph operators or counter hands to intelligent, educated working-class girls. The country's first Civil Service typist took up her post in the Department of Agriculture and Technical Instruction in 1901.

Nineteenth-century Belfast offered more opportunities for women's work than many British cities, especially from the mid-century with the rapid expan-

Belfast High Street.

sion of the linen industry. As a result, there were substantially more women in Belfast than men. In 1841 there were 38,000 females and 32,000 males; in 1901 the ratio was 188,000 to 162,000. Women worked in the linen industry, which in 1901 employed 24,000 females but only 7,000 males. Women were also found in large numbers in the clothing trades (11,000 compared with 4,000 males) and in domestic service, which employed almost 8,000 women and girls and provided 13 per cent of all female employment. Journalist Harriet Martineau, in her *Letters From Ireland*, published in 1852, wrote:

> In Belfast, the warehouses we saw were more than half peopled with women, engaged about the linens and muslins. And at the flax-works, near the city, not only were women employed in the spreading and drying, but in the rolling, roughing, and finishing, which had always till now been done by men. The men had struck for wages; and their work was given to girls, at 8d. per day.

Childhood as we understand it today as purely a time of play, of learning and amusement, was virtually non-existent for the majority of our Victorian ancestors. It was the preserve of the upper classes and the prosperous middles classes. Millions of children in the nineteenth century had the experience of working in a grown-up world by the time they were ten. William Tighe in his Survey of Kilkenny (1802) observed:

> The want of every kind of manufacture in which children of an early age might be usefully and profitably employed, occasions much of the poverty with which poor peasants here, who have young families, are obliged constantly to struggle. Neither the linens nor woollens made here, afford any occupation to children; nor have we any fabrics in which their little hands can find employment: the cotton manufacture carried on by spinning-jennies and other machinery, would supply this defect, if extensively established. By particular attention to the construction of the work-houses, and taking care to have a free circulation of air in them; and by a system that would oblige them to take sufficient exercise in the open air, and to use frequent bathings during the summer months, the health of children would not be impaired by being so employed; certainly without such an arrangement, sedentary occupations would be objectionable to children.

Both boys and girls went out to work because of the overwhelming necessity to get every penny into the household. Children had, of course, worked since time immemorial, but the new mechanised age created working and living conditions that were shocking. Factories, now steam powered and no longer dependent upon a steady water supply, moved into the towns and cities where there was a plentiful supply of child labour. Many factories were operated by apprentice pauper children from the nearby workhouses. They were housed in barrack-like apprentice houses so that they could not for long escape the confines of the factory. Only marginally better off were the so-called 'free' children who still lived at home in the surrounding slums.

The minimum age for starting at the spinning mill or weaving factory was eight years until 1874, when it was raised to ten years, eleven years in 1891 and twelve years in 1901. The law was openly flouted as only four inspectors were appointed to monitor this legislation, factory owners would continue to employ very young children. These juveniles or 'half-timers' attended school either in the mornings or afternoons, or on alternate days. Margaret Dixon McDougall commented after a visit to the National School in Tandragee:

> There are large schools, national schools, in this village, and the children over ten years of age, who work in the factory, go to school half time. They are paid at the rate of two-pence halfpenny a day for the work of the other half of the day – that is equivalent to five cents. The teachers of the schools informed me that, when the little ones came in the morning, as they did on alternate weeks, that they learned well, but when they came in the afternoon they were sleepy and listless. On that morning they had to rise at five o'clock.

Few occupations are more associated with the nineteenth century than that of chimney sweeps, also known as 'climbing boys'. They were probably the most wretched group of children during the later eighteenth and early nineteenth century. They were employed to climb up narrow chimney flues, dragging the brushes of their masters. It was estimated that there were 200 children employed climbing chimneys in Dublin in 1798. Their plight came to public attention in 1816 when a Dublin master sweep was accused of cruelty to a boy in his employment. During his trial he was shown to have flogged the child and burnt him with coals. When the wounds festered the child was dipped in cold water and then lashed and burned again. The child died shortly afterwards 'of a general mortification'. The sweep was sentenced to be publicly whipped and such was the crush of the crowd gathered to witness the spectacle, that eleven men, women and children were crushed to death when balustrades on the steps of the Royal Exchange collapsed.

A series of acts had, by the 1840s, limited the age at which a child could be apprenticed to the age of sixteen. But the law was largely ignored due to the absence of any means of enforcement. In 1863, the publication of *The Water-Babies*, a novel by Charles Kingsley, did much to raise public awareness about the gross mistreatment of children in this kind of employment through its central character, Tom, a child chimney sweep. But it was not until the 1870s that legislation required sweeps to be licensed and made it the duty of the police to enforce all previous legislation. It came too late to save one boy who died under horrible circumstances in Cork County Gaol in 1863. According to the *Cork Examiner* for 2 November of that year:

A BOY named Patrick Tansion [Tonson], about 14 years of age, was smothered in one of the chimneys of the County Gaol yesterday. He was apprentice of a sweep named Andrew M'Mahon, who has the contract of sweeping the chimneys of the gaol, and was on yesterday morning sent up one of the chimneys in the tower for the purpose of cleaning it. The chimney was rather narrow and when within some distance of the top the boy became jammed in it so he could neither go up nor down. In this position he was smothered, by the soot falling around him, before those beneath were aware of his danger. After he had been a short time in the chimney, his master became alarmed at his not returning, and called out to him. He received no answer, and on getting up found the unfortunate boy dead. The body was at once got down, and the police at the Victoria station were informed of the unhappy occurrence. Constable Real immediately proceeded to the gaol where he found M'Mahon, the deceased's employer. He asked who had sent the boy into the chimney, and on M'Mahon saying that he had done so, the constable took him into custody. M'Mahon was then carried before Mr. Leahy, J.P., and was committed to gaol until an inquest on the body of the boy should be held.

5

POOR LAW AND FAMINE

In *Our Mutual Friend*, Charles Dickens was scathing in his attack on the work-house system, declaring:

> I believe there has been no law so often infamously administered, no law so openly violated, no law habitually so ill-supervised. In the majority of the shameful cases of disease and death from destitution, that shock the public and disgrace the country, the illegality is quite equal to the inhumanity …

In spite of such criticism at home, the government introduced the English workhouse system to Ireland in 1838. Destitute poor who were previously granted relief at parish level were to be accommodated in new workhouses, where conditions were to be as unpleasant as was consistent with health.

Before the workhouses, the destitute were provided for by the parish authorities or private subscription. However, there remained plenty of pau-pers in the towns and cities to accost the unsuspecting visitor. The stranger waiting for a coach would swiftly become the centre of attention. Asenath Nicholson, the author of the *Bible in Ireland*, wrote of her visit to Tullamore in the mid-1840s:

> The chief centre of attraction was now where we stood, as I was a stranger. They attacked me with, 'God bless you', 'a penny, if you plase, lady', 'a ha'penny for a poor woman and child, whose father is dead this twelvemonth', 'one ha'p'orth for an old man', and 'the price of bread for a poor boy'; the boy grasping my clothes, and holding fast, in spite of my efforts to disengage myself the cries and importunities redoubling, while, like swarming bees, they sallied out from every quarter, till the crowd was immense.

In Dublin they followed customers into the stores to beg for money. Dr Edward Daniel Clarke, writing in the early 1820s observed:

> If you enter a fruit shop or tavern, a crowd of those poor creatures [beggars] infest the door, through which you must press your way, and deem yourself fortunate if you escape the detached parties of vermin which, wandering from the republic of their hair, hang on all parts of their bodies.

As many tourists found, there was a difference between the professional beggars of the cities and towns, and the peasant paupers of the country. In 1802 Robert Slade noted that cottiers planted their potatoes in whatever land they could find, then closed up their cabins and took to the road during July and August to beg until harvest time. Leitche Ritchie observed this practice in the 1830s:

> If you see … a ragged mother, with a baby on her back, and two or three ragged children at her heels, and more rarely, the ragged father bringing up the rear – if you see this melancholy cortege glide into the huts by the road-side … you may conclude with absolute certainty, that you have seen a family of pauper peasants.

They generally sought help from the neighbouring homes of those only marginally better off than themselves.

It was the possibility of a destitute old age that prompted early marriage among the peasantry. Writing in 1837, Elizabeth Charlotte noted:

> You must imagine, first, a state of society where the individual past work has no public asylum, no gratuitous provision of any sort whatever in store: the only prospect is that of having children grown up, who, through the powerful influence of natural feelings, cherished as most sacred among these people, will be constrained to shelter and sustain an infirm parent. Go where you will among the Irish poor, you may hear this motive expressly assigned for the very early marriages that they contract. If they deferred the engagement until they might have realized some little matter to begin the world with, their children would not be sufficiently grown to take charge of them, on the approach of the premature old age induced by their severe privations and over-work.

Partially as a response to the number of beggars and vagrants, the government passed the Irish Poor Law Act in 1838 which established workhouses in Ireland. Destitute poor who were previously granted relief at parish level were to be accommodated in the newly constructed workhouses. In England the units on which the poor law was administered were civil parishes, but in Ireland where the parishes had become outdated due to changes in population and settlement, the poor law unions were devised. The unions ignored traditional divisions, such as the county, barony and parish, and were centred on market towns where workhouses were built. One hundred and thirty-seven unions were created varying considerably in size, the largest ones being in the west of Ireland and the small ones in the eastern part of Ulster where the population was most dense.

The new workhouse-building project began in January 1839 with the arrival in Dublin of architect George Wilkinson. He had already designed a number of workhouses in England and Wales, including those at Thame, Stroud and Chipping Norton. His brief from the Poor Law Commissioners stated that, 'The style of building is intended to be of the cheapest description compatible with durability; and effect is aimed at by harmony of proportion and simplicity of arrangement, all mere decoration being studiously excluded.' The same design was used for all of the new workhouses. Workhouse construction proceeded with amazing speed and by April 1843 Wilkinson was able to report that 112 of the new workhouses were finished and 18 others were almost complete.

As the workhouses replaced local charity, beggars swarmed to those parts of the country where these forbidding structures had not yet been erected. Kohl noted this phenomenon when travelling through Ireland in the early 1840s:

> They command an extensive prospect over the country, and are the terror of the beggars, who prefer the independence of a mendicant's life to confinement in one of these houses. Some places, in which workhouses have not yet been erected, are at this moment swarming with beggars, who have there retreated to escape from these dreaded buildings.

He noted as he travelled into County Wicklow, 'In all the little towns through which we passed the people complained that they were now inundated with beggars, who had migrated from the larger towns where workhouses are erected, and where a stricter watch is kept over them.'

The Irish Poor Law system was designed to discourage all but the most needy paupers from applying to the workhouse for assistance. In their *Sixth Annual Report*, the Poor Law Commissioners admitted that it was no easy task to make conditions in the workhouse sufficiently bleak that it would deter only the most destitute:

It must be obvious to anyone conversant with the habits and mode of living of the Irish people that to establish a dietary in the workhouse inferior to the ordinary diet of the poor classes would be difficult, if not, in many cases, impossible; and hence it has been contended that the workhouse system of relief is inapplicable to Ireland.

They were forced instead to rely on the, 'regularity, order, strict enforcement of cleanliness, constant occupation, the preservation of decency and decorum, and exclusion of the irregular habits and tempting excitements of life' to deter only the most desperate from seeking refuge within the workhouse. The workhouse diet was modelled on that eaten by the poorest labourers in the country. Three basic menus were planned by the Commission, from which each Board of Guardians had to select one. Not surprisingly, the main food was potatoes, 3 or 3½lb, being the daily ration depending on the menu selected; something of a shock to the average labourer used to 10lb or 12lb or more daily.

The prescribed clothing for adult males was a coat and trousers 'of barragon', cap, shirt, brogues and stockings. For females it was a striped jerkin, a petticoat of 'linsy-woolsey' and another of stout cotton, a cap, a shift, shoes and stockings. Children were not provided with shoes and stockings on the grounds that they were not used to footwear. Edward Senior, an inspector with responsibility for twenty Northern unions, was alarmed by the condition of some of the children who he found in Ballymoney workhouse during the early part of 1848. He reported that:

There are about 30 children disabled by swelled feet the result of cold damp floors and want of shoes and stockings and that the medical officer concurred with me in the opinion that this is likely to promote disease. Delicate children should, I conceive, as in other houses, be shod. If the Guardians would go to the expense of providing wooden floors for the schoolrooms it would make the house much healthier as well as cleaner and save much in medicine and extra diet.

It was a fundamental rule of the workhouse system that 'no individual capable of exertion must ever be permitted to be idle in a workhouse and to allow none who are capable of employment to be idle at any time'. The men were employed breaking stones, grinding corn, working on the land attached to the workhouse or at other manual work about the house; the women at house duties, mending clothes, washing, attending the children and the sick, as well as manual work including breaking stones. The average day in the workhouse started at 7 a.m. at which time the inmates had to rise, dress in their workhouse clothes and then attend the central dining hall, where they waited for prayers to be read. The roll was called and they were inspected for cleanliness. They then lined up for their stirabout and milk. After breakfast the inmates were allocated work until late in the afternoon, when they had dinner of either potatoes or brown bread and soup. Inmates could not go to the dormitories until bedtime at 8 p.m. Kohl was not wrong when he commented, 'They are not intended simply as asylums for the poor, but also houses of correction, in which they may learn to put a still higher value on their golden freedom, accustom themselves to labour and learn to live without having recourse to begging.'

Such leisure time as they were allowed was strictly monitored. They were not allowed to play cards or any game of chance, nor were they permitted to smoke or drink any 'spirituous or fermented drink'. Inmates could see visitors only when accompanied by the Master, Matron or other duly authorised officer. Punishment for infraction of the rules was severe, as can be seen in the punishment books kept by the Masters of the workhouse. They were empowered to punish any pauper for a whole range of misdemeanours which included 'Making any noise when silence is ordered'; 'Not duly cleansing his person' and 'Playing at cards or any game of chance'. Punishments authorised for Armagh workhouse for 8 November 1845 included 'Maria McQuaid; disturbing the ward and swearing; to break stones for a week' and 'John Brown, Robert Minday, Thomas Martin and John Hamilton; abusing their new shoes; to go without shoes for a week and to be flogged.' The Master of Ballymoney workhouse reported that:

Thomas Smyth, James Brown and John McCord were caught pulling turnips and throwing them into the cess pools … the schoolmaster found Robert Quigley endeavouring to hang himself with a boy's belt tied to the front of one of the desks; he is a bad boy and tries to frighten the children by various means. Ordered that Smyth, Brown, McCord and Quigley be each flogged and put on the dietary of children for two weeks.

Horror of the workhouse was soon ingrained in the Irish peasant who would frequently endure any hardship rather than enter. Kohl put it down to the Irish love of freedom:

The Irish are thoroughly by nature as well as by habit, a migratory people, and fond of change. The Irishman would rather wander through the entire world seeking employment, than endure the discipline of a workhouse, so long as he is in possession of his health and strength. Imprisonment, and confinement of every kind, is to the Irishman more irksome than to the

Englishman. Consequently, even though he were much better off in a work-house than he could be at home, he would never enter one except in case of the most extreme distress ; and be will be sure to remain in it not a single moment longer than this distress continues.

Thomas Campbell Foster, writing in 1846, was less charitable, and put down the pauper's reluctance to go into the workhouse as being due to their unwill-ingness to wash:

> The chief objection, however, of the paupers against going into the workhouse, or remaining in it is, that they are compelled to wash themselves and keep themselves clean. When a three months' coating of dirt has been removed from their limbs, they go shivering about as if they had lost half their clothing, and no doubt do feel cold from the want of their accustomed covering. They are also forbidden to smoke, which is the greatest hardship to them.

The management of the workhouses was the responsibility of the Boards of Guardians, which were composed of elected representatives of the ratepay-ers in each union, together with ex-officio members including Justices of the Peace. The Guardians were answerable to local ratepayers and were expected to account for all monies spent in the administration of the workhouse. Sydney Godolphin Osborne pointed out in his *Gleanings in the West of Ireland* (1850):

> It may easily be conceived that the office of a Guardian is not a bed of roses in these Unions. A small body of police, I was told, are here regularly in attendance on the Board on admission days; applicants are very apt to be violent when refused altogether, or relieved in a way not according to their own views. It has happened that a Guardian has been severely wounded as he sat, by a stone thrown by one of these unruly spirits.

Landlords managed to maintain a large measure of control on Boards of Guardians during the early years. They served as ex-officio guardians and were able to assert a deal of influence over their tenants during elections. For much of Ireland's his-tory elections were fought along party lines with many contests reduced to power struggles between local priests and landlords with both national and local political issues a crucial factor. This was important because the Boards of Guardians were the only administrative body in rural areas with directly elected representatives. Throughout much of the country the Catholic middle classes came to dominate the boards as the century progressed and were later to use this experience as a step-pingstone to greater political ambitions; many went on to serve as MPs.

While the Guardians were legally responsible for the management of the workhouse and the collection and expenditure of money, the day-to-day running of the workhouse was carried out by a number of salaried officials. The staff consisted of a master, matron, clerk, chaplain, schoolmaster, medical officer, porter and additional assistants and servants that the Guardians deemed necessary. The Guardians were under pressure from the Poor Law Commissioners in London to discourage all but the most needy of paupers from applying to the workhouse for assistance. They therefore hired a number of paid officials who were chosen for their ability to discipline and regiment the paupers rather than for their humanitarian qualities.

In an attempt to prevent the religious issue dominating the administration of the Irish Poor Law, no person in Holy Orders or a regular Minister of any religious denomination could serve on the Boards of Guardians. Section 48 of the Irish Poor Relief Act specified that each workhouse should have 'one fit person' appointed chaplain to the workhouse, 'being in Holy Orders and of the Established Church, one other fit person being a Protestant Dissenter and one other fit person being a Priest or Clergyman of the Roman Catholic Church'. Chaplains were to celebrate divine service and to preach to the paupers every Sunday', they were to 'examine and catechise the children at least every month', and to record in a special book the progress of the children as well as the dates of their attendance at the workhouse. The clergy in many workhouses regarded each other with considerable hostility and a constant watch was kept to ensure that members of their flock were not poached by their opposite number. This is shown in an entry from the Chaplain's Book for Lurgan workhouse, dated 4 January 1848, written at the height of the Great Famine:

> On conversing today with Anne Jane Menary a Protestant who I had heard was in the habit of attending the service of the Roman Catholic Chaplain, I ascertained from her that she had gone to be cured from fits to which she was subject – I asked her what induced her to do so? She said "they all" told her it would make her well, and that when she went to the Roman Catholic Chaplain he said if she would say the things that he bid her & keep the rules he would cure her – this she tried for a while but not being able to do it right, she intends to become a Protestant again.

Difficulties in collecting the poor rate, together with people's general reluctance to enter these forbidding structures, meant that even by the summer of 1846, the workhouses were still only half full. Dunfanaghy workhouse in County Donegal, for example, contained only five inmates. This situation changed dramatically as the catastrophe of the Great Famine hit Ireland. The first sign of blight in Waterford and Wexford occurred in September 1845 and then spread rapidly until about half the country was affected. On 18 October 1845 the *Illustrated London News* reported that:

> Accounts received from different parts of Ireland show that the disease in the potato crops is extending far and wide, and causing great alarm amongst the peasantry. Letters from resident landlords feelingly describe the misery and consternation of the poor people around them, and earnestly urge the imperative necessity of speedy intervention on the part of the Government to ascertain the actual extent of the calamity, and provide wholesome food as a substitute for the deficient supply of potatoes.

More than one third of the crop was lost in 1845. In November, Prime Minister Sir Robert Peel spent £100,000 on Indian corn and meal in order to prevent soaring food prices in Ireland. Unlike potatoes, Indian corn required considerable preparation, and initial difficulties in grinding produced poorly refined meal causing digestive discomfort. In order to meet the growing distress, Peel established a relief commission and the formation of local committees was encouraged. Local voluntary contributions were supplemented by government grants, usually to the extent of two-thirds. Relief works, to which the government paid half the cost, were also set up to provide employment, for it was proposed to sell food rather than give it away.

By the beginning of 1846 the *Belfast New Letter* was convinced that the worst was over. The newspaper rejected talk of widespread famine; 'It is quite true that in some of our districts extreme scarcity prevails, as is invariably the case at this season; but the most active ingenuity of the famine-mongers has failed to magnify that scarcity into a greater than ordinary calamity.' The new Whig government, which took office in June 1846, also rejected talk of famine. The Prime Minister Lord John Russell, was committed to a *laissez faire* attitude, and believed it was wrong for the government to meddle in economic laws. He was convinced that the horror stories from Ireland were exaggerated. 'It must be thoroughly understood,' he declared, 'that we cannot feed the people.' The driving force in the new government's response to the famine was that of Sir Charles Trevelyan, Assistant Secretary to the Treasury. He was determined to ensure that state intervention would not undermine the principle that the government's purpose was to help local effort, not to supplant it.

The potato crop had failed before and people hoped that the next harvest would be all right. However, the blight returned in 1846 and this time the failure was complete. The speed with which the blight struck added to the horror. The Revd Samuel Montgomery, Rector of Ballinascreen in County Londonderry wrote an account in his parish register:

On the last days of July and the first six days of August 1846 the potatoes were suddenly attacked, when in their full growth, with a sudden blight. The tops were first observed to wither and then, on looking to the roots, the tubers were found hastening to Decomposition. The entire crop that in the Month of July appeared so luxuriant, about the 15th August manifested only blackened and withered stems. The whole atmosphere in the Month of September was tainted with the odour of the decaying potatoes.

The Whig government resolved that there would be no government buying; the supply of food was to be left exclusively to private enterprise. Relief was limited to public works and this time the government refused to meet half the cost, which was to be borne entirely by the rates. The idea was to force the Irish landlords to bear the cost.

Meanwhile winter set in, the harshest and longest in living memory. Hungry mobs roved the county and poured into the relief works. The numbers employed leapt from 30,000 in September to half a million in December. Horror stories began to emerge of the suffering of the Irish peasantry. A Special Reporter for *The Cork Examiner* visited Skibbereen in December 1846 and was appalled by what he saw:

dead bodies of children flung into holes hastily scratched in the earth, without a shroud or coffin – wives travelling ten miles to beg the charity of a coffin for a dead husband, and bearing it back that weary distance – a Government official offering the one-tenth of a sufficient supply of food at famine prices – every field becoming a grave, and the land a wilderness!

The situation was at its worst by February 1847 when great gales blew and the country was blanketed in thick snow. A fever epidemic also spread throughout the country. What people call 'Famine Fever' was in fact two separate diseases, typhus and relapsing fever. Other diseases such as scurvy spread particularly to those forced to depend on Indian meal which is lacking in vitamin C. The fear of infection caused people to refuse food and shelter to even their nearest neighbours. Fear of contracting fever through contact with the bodies of the dead (caused by the transfer of lice, though this was not known at the time) caused people to discontinue traditional burial ceremonies. Bodies lay for days in cabins which the survivors had deserted. Many others were found on the roadside, often with no means of identification.

Throughout Ireland those workhouses in operation began to fill up for the first time. The Board of Guardians in many parts of Ireland were soon overwhelmed by this cataclysm. The workhouse hospitals, designed to cope with a

Dungannon Board of Guardians. (Public Record Office of Northern Ireland)

very limited number of sick or injured inmates, were unable to cope with the level of distress as fever followed in the wake of famine. By 1847 almost every person admitted into workhouses was suffering from either dysentery or fever. Under such circumstances, separation became impossible. Disease spread, and the whole workhouse became one large infirmary, infecting not only the inmates but also the staff. During the first four months of 1847 more than 150 of the workhouse officers were attacked with disease, of whom 54 died, including seven clerks, nine masters, seven medical officers and six chaplains. There were casualties among the Boards of Guardians including the chairman of Lurgan Board of Guardians, Lord Lurgan, who died from the fever in 1847.

Sidney Goldolphin left a vivid description of a visit to the Limerick workhouse in his book *Gleanings in the West of Ireland*, published in 1850. He had visited the workhouse a year earlier and had found it clean and in good order. This visit was something of a shock:

> In the parent and auxiliary houses there was no less a number than 8,000 paupers; every department, except the fever hospital, shewed evident symptoms of gross neglect. I have no words with which I can give any real idea of the sad condition of the inmates of two large yards at the parent house, in which were a very large number of young female children; many of them clothed in the merest dirty rags, and of these they wore a very scanty allowance; they were in the dirt collected on their persons for many weeks; there

was not about them the slightest evidence of any the least care being taken of them; as they filed before me, two and two, they were a spectacle to fill any humane heart with indignation: sore feet, sore hands, sore heads; ophthalmia evident in the case of the great proportion of them; some of them were suffering from it in its very worst stage; they were evidently eat up with vermin – very many were mere skeletons ...

Goldolphin saw children die from the effects of starvation. He recalled after his visits to various infirmary wards in Ireland that he never heard one single child, suffering from famine or dysentery, utter a moan of pain. 'I have never heard one ask for food, for water – for anything', he recalled; 'two, three, or four in a bed, there they lie and die, if suffering, still ever silent, unmoved.'

The workhouses had nevertheless proved for many their only chance for survival. In their *Annual Report* of May 1848 the Irish Poor Law Commissioners underlined the importance of the workhouses in preventing a greater number of deaths during the Famine years:

Including the large number of inmates maintained in the workhouses, we may state that more than 800,000 persons are daily relieved at the charge of the poor-rates, consisting chiefly of the most helpless part of the most indigent classes in Ireland; and we cannot doubt that of this number a very large proportion are by this means, and this means alone, daily preserved from death through want of food ... Including the relief contributed by our Inspectors from the funds of the British Association, in certain distressed Unions, the entire number of persons provided with daily sustenance in Ireland, may be stated, in round numbers, to be 1,000,000, or about one eighth part of the whole population.'

As a direct result of the extraordinary circumstances brought about by the Famine, exceptional measures were introduced in Ireland in order to prevent the complete breakdown of the workhouse system. In June 1847, a separate Irish Poor Law Commission was set up and put in charge of further assistance under the Poor Relief (Ireland) Act. The 1847 Act also permitted the Board of Guardians to grant outdoor relief to the aged, infirm and poor, and to poor widows with two or more dependant children. The Enniskillen Boards of Guardians welcomed that fact that the Poor Law Commissioners had declared that able-bodied paupers were still to go to the workhouse which they felt sure would 'prevent imposition from idle able-bodied persons'.

On his tour through the west of Ireland in 1849, Osborne was not impressed by the outdoor relief system:

There can be no doubt but that out-relief is the cause itself of much mortality. The allowance, except where the small children are numerous enough to add from their quota some surplus, to the swelling of that of the adults, fall short of what can really support life, it is eked out by the free use of corn-weed, nettles and other weeds, and whatever else the parties can beg or take. Indian meal, however good a food when properly cooked, is far from wholesome when eat as these poor creatures eat it; few of whom have any means of properly cooking it; with but too many, from the almost raw state in which they eat it, it is little digested; however, they will hold out on it as long as nature will endure, for with it they have liberty.

Those obtaining outdoor relief could often go to desperate measures to ensure that they received an adequate amount. According to Osborne, 'It is a well known fact, that children dying, are sometimes buried privately by the parents so that the family may continue to draw their share of meal'.

As a means of reducing the numbers of destitute persons and lessening the burden of the crippling poor rate on the landowners, the Government gave its wholehearted supported to assisted emigration schemes. The Poor Relief Acts of 1838, 1843, 1847 and 1849 empowered the Boards of Guardians to raise such sums 'not exceeding the proceeds of one shilling in the pound' of the annual poor rate to 'assist poor persons who would otherwise have to be accommodated in the workhouse' to emigrate, preferably to the British Colonies. The Colonial Land and Emigration Commission was set up in England in 1840, under the control of the British Colonial Office, to organise and supervise emigration from both Britain and Ireland. The availability of emigration was constantly brought to the attention of the Boards of Guardians in circular letters issued by the Poor Law Commissioners. The representative of the Emigration Commission visited every workhouse in Ireland to inspect and select persons for emigration and those chosen were offered a free passage and supplied before departure with clothing and a little money to support themselves on arrival.

The Guardians also agreed that assisted emigration should be organised for inmates who had no means of providing support for themselves, such as single mothers with young children, or female orphans whose parents had abandoned them in the workhouse. This was largely an extension of a policy which was already in operation as workhouses in Ulster had for a number of years been arranging for inmates, both adult and children, to emigrate. A letter from Edward Senior, Assistant Poor Law Inspector, received by Ballymoney and other Ulster workhouses in April 1849, encouraged Guardians 'to send as emigrants to Canada any of the able-bodied inmates, especially females … in this move some of the permanent dead weight in the workhouse may be get rid of at a cost … of about five pounds or one year's cost of maintenance'.

Outside the workhouse, the Irish countryside was a place of horror. Travellers to Ireland at the time of the Great Famine noted its impact. While travelling along the southern side of the mountains near Bantry Bay the Revd John East was horrified to hear stories of packs of dogs feeding on the dead who were often laid to rest uncoffined and covered with a little earth:

> Hence the half-starved dogs, having tasted human carrion, are becoming insatiably eager for the horrid food. In another part of the country, they were lately discovered preying upon seven human bodies that had been deserted in a hedge. In vain did I hear a clergyman, in another place, apply to a police-officer to render aid in the destruction of the dogs. His reply was – 'The law is against us.' A clergyman told me that he had recently seen one of these animals with part of the body of a child in his mouth.

Travelling above a hundred miles by coach between Carlow and Cork, the Revd John Key was moved by 'the miserable condition of multitudes' which:

> forced itself into notice by visible facts, which spoke louder than even the deafening entreaties of mendicant crowds that beset the coach, and often had to be removed by force before it could proceed. There were towns in which the entire population seemed in motion, either to administer or to obtain relief; while one might see a pile of coffins, lodged against a carpenter's wall, exposed for sale, ready-made. In fact, I elsewhere passed through towns where this was the only mechanic trade carried on to advantage, and where the timber-merchant was heard to say, that he might close his yard and dismiss his sawyers, but for the demand for coffins. I saw the healthy dragging the sick and fevered, who ought to have been in bed, into view, to excite compassion. Parents would bring their children, mere masses of filth, disease, and breathing death, and almost thrust them into one's face or lap, while they themselves looked famine-struck. And yet the wretchedness visible without, was as nothing in comparison with that which appeared within, through every open cabin door.

The towns were filled with ragged and destitute people. On visiting Clifden in 1849, Sidney Godolphin Obsorne in his *Gleanings from the West of Ireland* (1850) confessed himself hardened to the poverty of the people, unlike his travelling companion:

Scavenger. (Henry Mayhews, *London Labour and the London Poor*)

My friend here again indulged himself in large investments in bread, to feed the
poor wretches he found in the street, and with the customary result; he soon
being forced from the pressure, to make a retreat at the rear of the shop. I cannot
wonder at the perseverance he displayed, he was new to Ireland; less hardened
than myself. From a window we got an opportunity of seeing, ourselves unseen,
some of the bread he had given consumed; there was no deceit in the way it
was devoured; more voracious reality, it would be hardly possible to conceive;
to see the fleshless arms grasping one part of a loaf, whilst the fingers – bone
handled forks – dug into the other, to supply the mouth – such mouths too!
With an eagerness, as if the bread was stolen, the thief starving, and the steps of
the owner heard; was a picture, I think neither of us will easily forget.

That was not an end to their tribulations caused by his friend's benevolence. On their way out of town they were followed by, 'a pack of famished creatures of all descriptions and sexes, set off in full chase after us; the taste of fresh bread, still inflamed the spirit of some; the report put others in hot hungry pursuit'. Their driver did his best but the road was up a very steep hill and they gained on the worried English passengers:

> No two luckless human brings were ever so hunted; no ravening wolves ever gave more open expression of their object – food. A little coaxing – my friend's; a little violence – my own; a little distribution of copper coin from both of us, at last rid us of the inconvenient, but natural result of an Englishman, with money in his pocket, and a baker's shop near, wishing in Ireland to feed some starving people.

By the beginning of the 1850s the numbers entering the workhouse began to drop for the first time since the beginning of the Famine. This was partially due to the 1851 Medical Charities Act. Before 1851 the sick had been able to obtain medical relief only in the workhouse hospitals, in county infirmaries and as out-patients in numerous dispensaries, some of which were established by local landlords. But these dispensaries were badly equipped. The 1851 Act rationalised this somewhat haphazard system. A Dispensary Committee was formed to take charge of each district. Each member of the committee, together with the Relieving Officer and Warden for the district, was empowered with issuing tickets enabling the poor persons to get medical treatment and medicine either at their own homes or at the dispensary. For nearly half a century the dispensary system became the essential framework of adequate medical care of the poor in Ireland.

The Great Famine of 1845-51 had brought about many changes to the Irish countryside. The ramshackle economy which had developed during the Napoleonic Wars had been destroyed by the potato blight. The persistent problem of unemployment had been eradicated. In 1851 the population was six and a half million, two million less than the estimated population of 1845, a million having emigrated and another million dead as a result of starvation and disease. However, already the pattern of Irish agriculture was beginning to emerge, with family farms engaged in mixed tillage and livestock production.

The Irish Poor Law continued for a century while the shadow of the workhouse hung over most members of the working class and even some of the middle class, including orphaned families and foundling children, women with large families who were suddenly widowed, the old and infirm – all dreaded incarceration the forbidding walls of the workhouse. As the century progressed, the function of the workhouse gradually changed. It became an institution for the old, sick and vagrants. Additional powers were given to the Boards of Guardians under the Act of 1862. This Act declared that it was 'expedient to extend to cases of sickness or accident the powers which the guardians now possess, in regard to fever cases'. This was a very important development as it opened the workhouse hospitals to sick people who were not destitute. The Act also led the Poor Law into a whole new service – that of boarding out children. Prior to this act, orphaned or deserted children could only be maintained in the workhouse but a series of investigations showed that the mortality among children admitted to the workhouse was excessive. In 1859 the Poor Law Commissioners admitted that:

> A great rate of mortality prevails everywhere, as well as in workhouses, in the class of children under two years of age; but that rate is much increased in the workhouses in regard to the children who are without mothers; as it is found impossible to procure for them, in the workhouse, that kind of substitute for maternal care and solicitude which is necessary for them at that age.

For the older children the emphasis was on 'literary and industrial training', both inside the workhouse and in the industrial schools outside. A national primary school system had been established in 1831; however, the Poor Law Commissioners were hostile to workhouse children being educated outside the institute because 'irregularity and laxity of discipline would probably arise from the children being permitted to leave the workhouse daily'. A schoolmaster and schoolmistress were appointed to the workhouse, the Guardians themselves selecting the teachers and fixing their salaries. The workhouse schools were, unlike the National Schools, interdenominational.

It was generally accepted that if the unions were to be relieved of the responsibility of the children it would be through their employment as labourers or domestic servants. The regulations for the management of the workhouses provided that a minimum of only three hours should be spent daily educating the children. Instead the regulations provided for occupational instruction to fit the children for service and to train them 'to habits of usefulness, industry and virtue'. In 1848 the Guardians were empowered to purchase land which was to be used as farms to train children in agricultural work. Seasonal work could also be found. In some workhouses there was a practice of hiring out children to farmers in the spring, summer and autumn months. But it proved difficult to secure positions for workhouse girls. The Poor Law Commissioners encouraged the instruction of girls in embroidery and other ornamental work. In Belfast, owing to the many local factories, the demand for workhouse children exceeded the supply. But in other areas, particularly the south and west of Ireland there was little demand for pauper children.

For the remainder of the nineteenth century the workhouse remained a place where only the most desperate would willingly enter. Margaret Dixon McDougall on her visit to the workhouse in Manor Hamilton in 1882 was appalled by what she saw:

> We passed the closed doors of the casual ward, where intending inmates were examined for admittance, and casuals were lodged for the night. Every door was unlocked to admit us and carefully locked behind us, conveying an idea of very prison-like administration. The able-bodied were at work, I suppose, for few were visible except women who were nursing children. There was a large number of patients in the infirmary wards. One man whose bed was on the floor was evidently very near the gate we all must enter. He never opened his eyes or seemed conscious of the presence of a stranger. I noticed a little boy lift the poor head to place it easier. I saw no one whom I could imagine was a nurse … The children in this workhouse were pretty numerous. They demanded something from me with the air of little footpads. The women were little better. I was told, pretty imperatively, to look in my pockets. One woman rushed after me half way up stairs as if she would compel a gift.

She rushed from the workhouse and later reflected:

> I think it is hard for struggling poverty to go down so far as to take shelter in the workhouse. It must be like the bitterness of death. I cannot imagine the feeling of any human beings when the big door clashes on them, the key turns, and they find themselves an inmate of the workhouse at Manor Hamilton. I do not wonder that the creatures starving outside preferred to suffer rather than go in.

6

LAW AND ORDER

Nineteenth-century Ireland was often a disturbed and violent place. In a century which saw the government intervene in education, social welfare and land reform, its chief concern remained the preservation of law and order. Ireland was perceived in the popular English press as a lawless country, rife with agrarian crime and assassination. On the other hand, as many visitors to the island were keen to point out, the inhabitants were a peaceable lot. John Gamble, visiting the north of Ireland in 1812 commented:

> There is not in the universe a country more free from violence or robbery than the North of Ireland. Highway robbery is almost unknown. House-breaking certainly does occur, but not often. The great thefts are horse-stealing and bleach-green robbing. In several counties not a man has been executed for many years.

A strong army presence was a feature of nineteenth-century Ireland. Ostensibly it protected Ireland from foreign invasion; in fact it also assisted county authorities against internal discontent. Sir Robert Peel commented that without the army, 'the whole framework of civilised society would be threatened with dissolution', so great was the popular antipathy to civilian authorities. The size of the garrison varied depending on social and political conditions: in 1841 it stood at 11,000, by the end of the decade, with the Young Ireland Rising it numbered 27,000. Regiments and detachments of soldiers with their baggage trains were a regular feature of Irish roads until after the middle of the nineteenth century and the coming of the railways.

Most of the soldiers' time was spent in the daily round of drills, parades, fatigues and marches. Their chief responsibility was to assist the civil power in preserving the public peace. This involved supplying detachments to escort

prisoners, to protect sub-sheriffs executing judgments against defaulting tenants
and tithe payers, to guard wrecks, to keep the peace at fairs and race meetings
and at elections, and to search the country for arms. As a result, regiments were
frequently split up into numerous small detachments, scattered at different
posts, there being at one time more than 400 military stations in Ireland. The
army could also be a source of friction, as shown by the following extract from
the *Cork Examiner*, 8 May 1878:

THE RESERVES.
SERIOUS AFFRAY IN DUBLIN.
A serious affray occurred last evening at the Harcourt-street railway station,
Dublin, between the Wicklow army reserve detachment, and some policemen.
The soldiers were hanging about the terminus awaiting the remainder of their
comrades to proceed to Kingsbridge for Limerick. All were under the influence
of drink, and one struck a policeman several times, and a general melee began.
The policemen, numbering about half a dozen, drew their batons. Both sides
were reinforced by civilians, and a free fight lasted for about twenty minutes,
when a posse of policemen came up and took the ringleaders into custody.
About a dozen soldiers were carried to the nearest hospital, none seriously
injured. Several policemen were much hurt. A large crowd thronged the street,
completely stopping the traffic, and the excitement of the spectators was intense.

In order to control endemic agrarian violence as well as dangerous political
movements, parliament frequently resorted to laws suspending civil liberties
for designated periods of time. First introduced in 1796, the Insurrection Act
imposed the death penalty (replaced in 1807 by transportation for life) on persons administering illegal oaths. It also allowed government to proclaim specific
districts as disturbed, thereby imposing a curfew, suspending trial by jury, and
giving magistrates sweeping powers of search and detention. From 1833 a new
type of Coercion Act took over as the standard response to Irish disorders. Like
the earlier Insurrection Act, this empowered the Lord Lieutenant to proclaim
a district as disturbed, permitting the imposition of a curfew and other restrictions, as well as detention without trial for up to three months. It differed from
the Insurrection Act in providing for trial by military courts rather than magistrates in special session.

As the nineteenth century progressed, law and order became more and more
a policing matter. Despite a series of acts of parliament passed during the eighteenth century, the Irish police force at the time of the Act of Union of 1800 was
still composed only of small groups of sub-constables. These part-time policemen, appointed by the grand juries, were few in number and poorly paid out

of the county funds. In 1814 Sir Robert Peel, then Chief Secretary in Ireland, created the Peace Preservation Force, popularly known as 'Peelers' which could be called upon by the Lord Lieutenant for use in a district that had been 'proclaimed' as a disturbed area. This force proved inadequate and in 1822 the County Constabulary was established to maintain law and order throughout the rest of the country while the Peace Preservation Force worked in proclaimed districts.

Under the reforming Irish Executive of 1835-41 the Under Secretary, Thomas Drummond remodelled the system yet again. He absorbed all the existing police forces into a new body called the Irish Constabulary under an Inspector-General in Dublin. Power to appoint and discharge members of the force, to make rules and to fix salaries was vested in the Lord Lieutenant of Ireland. The Irish Constabulary was responsible for the preservation of law and order throughout the country with the exception of Dublin and Belfast which retained their own police forces.

By 1836 the Irish Constabulary had grown to around 5,000 men and by 1841 this had risen to over 8,000. Elizabeth George, in her *Letters from Ireland* (1837), found the new force very different to the one she was used to in London:

> In occasionally naming the police, I must guard you against the mistake of identifying them with those peaceable-looking gentry, who, with blue coats well buttoned up, and respectable round hats, perambulate the streets of London, apparently not only inoffensive but defenceless too; and whose chief business, as a casual observer would surmise, is to answer the frequent queries of bewildered pedestrians, at a loss whether the right turning or the left will sooner bring them to their destination. The police force of Ireland present a far different aspect: their uniform is dark green, altogether of military fashion, with regimental cap, broad black belt, short musket, cartouche-box, and bayonet. The officers, or chief and deputy chief constables as they care called, wear swords. This is one of the saddening characteristics of poor Ireland.

The police force was a very visible presence in even the most remote parts of the country. 'One thing that impresses a stranger here', wrote Margret Dixon McDougall in the 1880s:

> is the number of policemen; they are literally swarming everywhere. Very dandified as to dress and bearing, very vigilant and watchful about the eyes, with a double portion of importance pervading them all over as men on whom the peace and safety of the country depend. These very dignified conservators of the peace are most obliging. Ask them any question of locality, or for direction anywhere, and their faces open out into human kindness and interest at once.

Patron Day. (John Barrow, *Tour Round Ireland: Through the Sea-Coast Counties, in the Autumn of 1835*)

Members of the force, who were mainly Catholic, were recruited from among the tenant farmer class and were removed to distant stations. The force was unpopular in many areas because it was used to assist at evictions and because it supplied Dublin Castle with most of its intelligence information. The duties of the Constabulary were gradually extended. At first it was solely concerned with keeping the peace, a duty which could entail the suppression of armed rebellion, sectarian riots or agrarian disturbances. Later it inherited the functions of the Revenue Police, made inquiries on behalf of departments of state, collected agricultural statistics, enforced the fishery laws and performed a variety of duties under the laws relating to food and drugs, weights and measures, explosives and petroleum. Members of the force also acted as enumerators at the censuses of population. Sir Francis Head visited several barracks during the early 1850s. At Ballynakill near Clifden he found:

> On my asking him what were his principal duties, he readily replied, 'Executing warrants generally, and especially for poor-laws; arresting those who have absconded from workhouses with the clothes thereof, besides often leaving their families behind; escorting prisoners by night and by day ; patrolling from two to four miles from the station; going to fairs and ' patrons,' on the requirement of a magistrate, where disturbances are expected; attending quarter sessions, assizes, and at elections, if called upon.

The riots in Belfast. (*Illustrated London News*, 19 June 1886)

For this work they were poorly paid. There were no recognised off-duty periods or annual leave and a constable was confined to barracks at night. He could only marry after seven years' service and then his proposed bride had to meet with the approval of the authorities. A constable could not vote in elections. It was also forbidden for policeman and their wives to sell produce, take lodgers or engage in certain forms of trade.

By the end of the nineteenth century, there were a total of around 1,600 barracks dotted around the Irish countryside with four or five policemen living in each barrack. The sergeant had to ensure that the barracks were clean: the walls were regularly freshly whitewashed; the constables' bedsteads and blankets were neatly rolled up; the floors of the barracks to be spotlessly clean. The local barracks was a popular source of information for many well-intentioned visitors to Ireland during the period. Mr and Mrs Hall visited the police station at Ballyneed, a village near Dunmanway in the 1840s:

It contained five men, strong and active fellows; the rooms were all whitewashed, the little garden was well-cultivated and free from weeds. The men slept on iron bedsteads, and the palliasses, blankets, pillows, etc., were neatly rolled up and placed at the head of each. The fire-arms and bayonets, each as polished as a mirror, were hung up over each bed and the floors were as clean 'as a new pin'. Each man had his small box at his bed foot. All was in as perfect order as if all had been prepared in this little out-of-the-way place for the accustomed call of the inspector … In this barrack the men were all bachelors; but it is usual to assign one married man with his wife to each barrack — the wife, of course, arranging the rooms, and providing the meals of the men who always mess together.

Visitors were impressed by the calibre of men recruited. Sir John Forbes commented:

> They are, I believe, the picked men of Ireland; and being so, I verily believe it scarcely an exaggeration to say that they are also the picked men of mankind. They are not merely all tall, well-grown, and muscular, but they are almost all … well-knit, of fine carriage, and of handsome countenances.

S. Reynolds Hole, Dean of Rochester, who visited Ireland in the early 1890s agreed:

> There is no exaggeration in stating, that if a regiment could be formed from the Irish constables, it would be the finest regiment in arms. See them wherever you may, they are, almost without exception, handsome, heroic. Picked men, and admirably trained, they are as smart, and clean, lithe, and soldier-like, as the severest sergeant could desire.

W.H. Richardson, who toured the North of Ireland in 1880 agreed. 'They are all tall, broad-shouldered, handsome, and, as a rule, good-natured fellows, and we invariably received courtesy and information from them.' He thought that the combination of military and legal training they received made them 'very superior to the English police.'

In September 1867, as a result of its loyalty during the Fenian Rising, the Constabulary was renamed the Royal Irish Constabulary and so became the first 'Royal' police force in the British Empire. Queen Victoria also granted the 'Royal Irish Constabulary' the harp, crown and shamrocks of 'The Most Illustrious Order of St. Patrick'. The importance of a large police presence in Ireland was acknowledged by Samuel Hussey in his *Reminiscences of an Irish Land Agent* (1904):

> There is a story of an English tourist seeking for information about the distressful country, he being at Tallaght near Dublin.
> He asked the carman whether there were many Fenians about.
> 'A terrible lot, your honour,' replied the fellow.
> 'I suppose a thousand?' the tourist suggested, some what apprehensively.
> 'That is so, and twenty thousand more', answered the carman without hesitation.
> 'Are they armed?' was the next question.

'They are that, and finely into the bargain.'

'And are they prepared to come out?' the tourist being much perturbed, and thinking it would be his duty to write to *The Times*.

'Prepared to come out in the morning, your honour.'

'And why don't they do so?' with English common sense.

'Begorra, because maybe if they did, the constabulary would put them in jail.'

There existed, nevertheless, a class who cared little for the police as noted by the Revd William Murphy O'Hanlon in his *Walks Among the Poor of Belfast*, (1853) which shocked Belfast public opinion. Of Barrack Lane he wrote:

> here every kind of profligacy and crime is carried on, despite the police, who seem to be little terror to evil-doers in this quarter. Passers of base coin, thieves, and prostitutes, all herd here together in this place as in a common hell, and sounds of blasphemy, shouts of mad debauch, and cries of quarrel and blood, are frequently heard here through the livelong night, to the annoyance and terror of the neighbourhood … It is the practice, as we were informed, of these miscreants to frequent the docks, and, having caught sailors, like unwary birds, in their toils [*sic*], to allure them to these pitfalls, where they are soon peeled and plundered.

Throughout the nineteenth century the activities of the 'criminal classes', to use a term which was in vogue during the middle of the nineteenth century, was given a great deal of column inches in newspapers. Most offenders were young males, and most offences were petty thefts. The most common offences committed by women were linked to prostitution and were essentially 'victimless' crimes: soliciting, drunkenness, drunk and disorderly, vagrancy. Domestic violence rarely came before the courts. It tended to be committed in the private sphere of the home. Among some working-class communities it continued to have a degree of tolerance, while amongst other classes the publicising of such behaviour even, perhaps especially, in the courts, would have been regarded as bringing a family's reputation into disrepute.

One group routinely subjected to harassment of the police was the resident population of vagrants and beggars. In April 1820 the police commissioners in Belfast blamed the 'alarming' rise in robberies and thefts in the town in the previous two or three years on the vagrant population. In 1809 a House of Industry was set up with the aim of suppressing begging in Belfast streets and the police were frequently reminded by the commissioners to arrest beggars, especially children.

Juvenile delinquents were responsible for a large share of crime. *The Belfast News Letter* stated in March 1853 that 'small thieves and small thefts' occupied most of the criminal proceedings in Belfast's courts. In June 1826 John Cullen was sentenced to one year in prison with hard labour for stealing six silk shawls from a Bridge Street shop. He was only six years old, and was so small that he could not be seen in the dock during his trial. John McClure, aged fourteen in August 1853, who had sixteen convictions for theft, served ten prison terms and was whipped six times; James Kennedy, a 'young scoundrel' with nine convictions for theft before 1854, was so well known to the police that he 'could not safely pursue his profession any longer in his customary garbs, and had, therefore, donned the attire of a seaman'; twelve-year-old Robert Wilson, had by February 1856 served twenty-two months in prison for theft and other offences.

Young children were subjected to the same system of punishment as their elders, as shown in the following entry for the *Anglo-Celt* for 4 November 1852:

> Mark FLAHERTY, an urchin scarcely over twelve years old, concealed him-
> self and committed a robbery in the shop of Mr. James O'BRIEN, grocer,
> 33 Lower Ship-street. The only mode by which the culprit could have con-
> trived to secret himself in the palace was by stealing in unobserved sometime
> during the business hours on the evening before, and stowing himself away
> amongst the casks and tea chests, thus remained concealed until the family
> had gone to rest. He was sentenced to be privately whipped and imprisoned
> for two months with hard labour.

Some children drifted into crime because of the death of a parent, which often meant that the only alternative was the workhouse. Daniel Montgomery a 'little boy' who was caught stealing delft in February 1855, avoided a prison sentence when he explained that his mother was dead and his father was 'away at the wars', leaving him without means of support. Twelve-year-old John McManus of West Street, Belfast, who had already spent four months in prison before his court appearance in October 1859 on a charge of stealing a pair of socks and assaulting Constable McKnight in the police court, explained that his father was dead and that he was the sole support of his sick mother and his little brother.

The Industrial Schools Act 1857 enabled magistrates to send children found begging or needing care and protection to Industrial Schools to learn a trade. Industrial Schools were similar to National Schools except that they were required to spend only two hours a day on literary work and the rest on industrial training. The Reformatory Schools Act of 1868 turned industrial schools into reformatories for juvenile offenders. Based on the English model, they received convicted children under the age of twelve while convicts aged between twelve and sixteen were dispatched to reformatories. By 1900 there were seventy such schools, with a capacity for over 8,000 children, operating in Ireland, entirely under religious control yet financed by the state. Children were sent to the appropriate reformatory schools as dedicated by their religious background. As with the workhouses, disputes frequently arose when children were sent to the reformatory of a different religion. In a letter to the *Irish Times*, dated 29 December 1860, the writer complained that fourteen-year-old James Tyrrell, a Protestant, had been sent to a Catholic reformatory. Under the emotive heading 'New Mode of Kidnapping – Reformatory Schools' the writer complained that no one had enquired of the delinquent's mother as to his religious background:

> I suppose our trustworthy police conducted the inquiry. Of course, they could find no proof of his Protestantism – somebody told him it would be better for him to go with his companions to Glencree. He might have heard that it was a beautiful place, where he would have the best of treatment, plenty of play, a band of music, &c., &c. Glowing must be the picture of a poor, friendless little boy, trembling before his judge, and, possibly, receiving some looks of sympathy and whispers of consolation from the policeman, who held him by the collar, and whose feelings for young Protestants had been strongly excited when the worthy official attended his usual course of instruction from the revd. Fathers of Gardiner Street chapel.

The writer also alleged that during the previous three weeks 'four boys – named Preston, Gordon, Curry and Lambert – had also been sent to reformatories. Those sound very like Protestant names, but when brought up to custody of the police, they were all Roman Catholics!'

John Fagan, the inspector of reformatories and industrial schools, reported in 1867 that of 1,410 children admitted to the schools that year, 904 had been classified as children found begging in public. The inspector claimed that in a large number of cases this situation had been deliberately contrived by destitute parents in order to qualify their children for admission. They were more appropriately objects for workhouse charity but such was the unpopularity of such a fate amongst the poor that the industrial schools were considered a more desirable alternative. Life in the industrial school could nevertheless be harsh, as witnessed by an account which appeared in the *Belfast News Letter* on 21 May 1880:

> A young lad named Peter Corrigan was put forward in custody of Constable Campton, charged with having absconded from St. Patrick's Roman Catholic Industrial School … James Collins, superintendent of the school, said that the prisoner was a very bad boy, and was very unwilling to attend to any order he

received. He had escaped at a very early hour on Monday morning, and must have gone out through one of the dormitory windows. Constable Campton said that after the prisoner was put into the cells some other prisoners drew his attention to the fact that he was complaining of his back being sore, and that he had been badly abused in the school. Witness examined him and found some marks on his back. Dr. A ... examined him and reported that the marks were very slight. Mr Collins said that the prisoner had attempted to escape on Sunday evening and he beat him on the shoulders with a small cane. The punishment awarded was not so severe as the prisoner's conduct warranted.

The boy was sentenced to fourteen days imprisonment, at the end of which he was to be sent to a Roman Catholic Reformatory.

Prior to the Suicide Act of 1961 it was a crime to commit suicide and anyone who attempted and failed could be prosecuted and imprisoned, while the families of those who succeeded could also potentially be prosecuted. In part that reflected religious and moral objections to suicide as self-murder. Judges nevertheless often exercised an element of mercy as the following extract from the *Belfast News Letter* from 5 September 1888 demonstrates:

John Conroy was charged by Constable Cuddy with having attempted to commit suicide on Monday evening last at McDonnell Street. It appeared from the evidence of the prisoner's son and mother that he had asked for a razor on the evening in question to cut his throat. On being refused, he had got a muffler and a number of handkerchiefs, and attempted to strangle himself. The witness believed that the prisoner's mind had been affected by the death of a son some twelve months ago. Dr Torrens examined the accused, and stated that in his opinion the prisoner was a fit object of a lunatic asylum. Their Worships gave an order for the committal of the accused to the lunatic asylum.

Infanticide is another regular feature of Victorian newspapers. These young women had given birth to illegitimate babies which made them outcasts in their own communities. Such women found guilty of infanticide were likely to be confined within the walls of the nearest lunatic asylum. According to the annual reports on Dundrum from the inspectors of lunacy, such cases evoked a degree of sympathy:

Great commiseration is, no doubt, due to many who come within this category; for we can fully imagine how shame and anguish must weigh on an unfortunate and betrayed female, with enfeebled system, what strong temptations induce her to evade the censure of the world in the destruction of the evidence of her guilt, by a crime that outrages her most powerful instinct, maternal love of offspring. The thought of such a fearful exposure no doubt may lead to some sudden and impulsive act, for which, as generally happens, she is judged with the utmost leniency.

Another crime which caused public distress in the first half of the nineteenth century was that of body snatching. Before the Anatomy Act of 1832, the only legal supply of corpses for anatomical purposes were those condemned to death and dissection by the courts. Such sentences did not provide enough subjects for the medical schools and private anatomical schools, many of whom were prepared to accept cadavers without asking too many difficult questions. They were helped by the fact that stealing a corpse was only a misdemeanour at common law, not a felony, and was only punishable with a fine and imprisonment, rather than transportation or execution. The trade was a sufficiently lucrative business to run the risk of detection, particularly as the authorities tended to ignore what they considered a necessary evil. The general public took a very different view, and newspapers were suitably appalled by such activities as can be seen in an account which appeared in the *Ballyshannon Herald and Donegal Advertiser* in January 1832:

> Body Snatching.--Yesterday there was discovered in the Steam-boat yard the dead body of a man, packed up in a new box, and directed to 'Captain Walker, Glasgow, care of the Steward of the Foyle.' It appears from the information of Andrew Cameron, taken in the Mayor's Office by John Dysart, Esq. that the body found was that of his brother, James Cameron, who died on Friday week, aged 82, and on the Monday following was buried in Castlederg church-yard – that on the day following he was informed the body had been stolen away – and that on repairing to the church yard, and having the coffin opened, he ascertained that this was the fact: and that he had good reason for believing that the said body was in the possession of Robert M'Kelvy, carrier now in this city. This information led to the detection, and from evidence afterwards adduced, it appeared that M'Kelvy did not bring the box, but the servant of a Mr. Adams, of Castlederg, whose son is a Medical Student in Glasgow College. Informations have been lodged against the servant, and constables have been sent in quest of him. The investigation was adjourned till one o'clock this day, (Saturday), while M'Kelvy is under security to appear. The servant has been apprehended.

Murder cases were followed with great enthusiasm in the papers, the more sensational the better. The death of Bridget Cleary, killed by her husband in 1895, had enough grizzly details to cause a national outcry. Her death is notable for several peculiarities such as the stated motive for the crime. It was her husband's belief that she had been abducted by fairies with a changeling left in her place; he claimed to have killed only the changeling. The gruesome nature of the case – Cleary's body was set on fire, either causing or immediately following her death – prompted extensive press coverage at the time. Michael Cleary was found guilty of man-slaughter, and spent fifteen years in prison. Bridget Cleary's death has remained famous in popular culture and is celebrated in an old nursery rhyme with the lines, 'Are you a witch, or are you a fairy, Or are you the wife of Michael Cleary?'

Twice a year the common law judges went on circuit to try major civil and criminal cases, including murder, infanticide, rape, robbery, burglary and arson, at the assizes in county towns. The selection of cases to go before them was the responsibility of the county grand jury. The judge was received with great pomp and treated to lavish hospitality. The novelist William Makepeace Thackeray left an account of the assize at Waterford in his *Irish Sketchbook*:

> The witness is here placed on a table instead of a witness-box; nor was there much farther peculiarity to remark, except in the dirt of the court, the absence of the barristerial wig and gown, and the great coolness with which a fellow who seemed a sort of clerk, usher, and Irish interpreter to the court, recom-mended a prisoner, who was making rather a long defence, to be quiet. I asked him why the man might not have his say. 'Sure,' says he, 'he's said all he has to say, and there's no use in any more.' But there was no use in attempting to convince Mr. Usher that the prisoner was best judge on this point: in fact the poor devil shut his mouth at the admonition, and was found guilty with perfect justice.

The Quarter Sessions in each county were presided over by two or more Justices of the Peace. The sessions took place in the weeks around the dates of Epiphany (6 January), Easter (moveable), Midsummer (24 June) and Michaelmas (29 September) and took their names. They dealt with less serious crimes such as bigamy, assault, concealment of birth, bribery, criminal damage, prostitution, theft and vagrancy. Nineteenth-century justice was often arbitrary in nature as can been seen in the following extract from the *Belfast News Letter*:

BELFAST QUARTER SESSIONS
Tuesday, 9th July 1839
Charles Magennis, for stealing a coat, at Belfast, on 12th June, the property of Francis McIlwaine. Pleaded guilty; four months' imprisonment.
Thomas Hunter, for stealing a piece of bacon, on 12th June, the property of John Finlay. Guilty; seven years' transportation.

John McBride, for having in his possession a grate, on the 4th June last; same stolen from J. Hunter. Pleaded guilty; six weeks' imprisonment.

Margaret McKeown, for stealing a cap and cloak, at Belfast, on 13th June last, from Matilda Patterson. Pleaded guilty; two months' imprisonment.

Michael Dyer, for having in his possession a piece of baize, at Belfast, on 29th May, the property of Isabella Toole; same having been stolen. Seven years' transportation.

Sarah Green, for stealing two half-crown pieces and a sovereign from Hiram Griffith, on the 24th June last. Three months' imprisonment.

The Petty Sessions Court was the lowest rung of the judicial structure, its purpose to adjudicate on what were considered minor offences which made of the vast bulk of civil and criminal cases. These included offences such as wandering cattle, drunk and disorderly, disputes amongst neighbours, keeping a dangerous dog and school attendance. The Petty Sessions Court was presided over by two or more unpaid Justices of the Peace, or by a single paid (stipendiary) Magistrate without the need for a jury. Each court met daily, weekly or monthly, depending on the volume of cases to be heard. William Makepeace Thackeray visited Roundstone Petty Sessions in 1842:

> the Sessions-room at Roundstone, is an apartment of some twelve feet square, with a deal table and a couple of chairs for the accommodation of the magistrates, and a testament with a paper cross pasted on it to be kissed by the witnesses and complainants who frequent the court. The law-papers, warrants, &c., are kept on the Sessions-clerk's bed in an adjoining apartment, which commands a fine view of the courtyard, where there is a stack of turf, a pig, and a shed beneath which the magistrate's horses were sheltered during the sitting. The Sessions-clerk is a gentlemen 'having', as the phrase is here, both the English and Irish languages, and interpreting for the benefit of the worshipful bench.

Court sessions in any small Irish town were a great source of popular entertainment. Local 'characters' frequently played a starring role supported by their amused neighbours, as seen in the *Ballina Chronicle*, 1 May 1850:

CITY POLICE COURT
THE FAIRIES – At the city Limerick Police court on Thursday, a lad named Cornelius Hennessey, arrested as a vagrant, told the presiding Magistrate he had been for some time with the fairies!
Magistrate – Who are the fairies?

Prisoner – The 'good people', whose souls the Almighty lets live upon earth, though their bodies are buried – they took me away from my father's house, and in a hurling match they broke my leg. (laughter)

A Policeman – Though young that lad is, your worship, he is most incorrigible – breaks window glass and plunders bread-shops – he has a name for every day of the week.

Magistrate – If I let you off will you go back to your father?

Prisoner – How can I, sir? Sure there is a fairy at home at my place, and my father thinks he is his son; as he says he don't know me. (great laughter).

Magistrate – I'll send you back to the 'good people' so. (a laugh).

Prisoner – I wouldn't know where to find them now, sir. (much laughter).

Magistrate – I believe not, but you shan't put a finger in my eye. You are a regular juvenile trickster, and I'll punish you.

Prisoner – I am satisfied if it is by giving me enough to eat, your honour. (roars of laughter).

Magistrate – I sentence you to 21 days imprisonment, at hard labour on the treadmill.

Prisoner – Very well, sir, I used to practice a little that way with the fairies (loud laughter) – When you go to them that you may break your shins on the treadmill (immoderate laughter).

The delinquent was then committed.

Those who paid the ultimate price for their crimes during the early nineteenth century were executed publically in the locality and their bodies left hanging by the roadside as a powerful deterrent. As early as 1812 John Gamble recounted a story with typical gallows' humour:

The murderer was executed near the road, and the body hung in chains. A circumstance half ludicrous, half melancholy, occurred about a fortnight afterwards. The gaoler, who had superintended the execution, returning late at night from a fair in the neighbourhood, made a bet with some people that were along with him, that he would ride up to the gallows, and would give the body a blow with his whip. This he performed; but a poor foolish creature happening to be asleep at the foot of the tree, started up, and called to him 'Dinna strike him now, man, he is dead, and can da ye na harm.' The gaoler was so alarmed, that he set off at full gallop; and, without proceeding far, dropped off his horse and expired.

Executions were public events and well attended but not everyone was immune to the horror of such a spectacle according to the *Belfast News Letter* for 17 August 1849:

EXECUTION AT ENNISKILLEN –The two unfortunate men, Wilson and Kerr, who were found guilty at last assizes for Fermanagh, of the murder of John Wilson, the brother of one of the culprits, were executed, on the 9th inst., in front of the county gaol. They were both penitents, and in their confession exonerated the servant boy, Cathcart, who was also convicted as being an accomplice in the murder, upon the testimony of his fellow-servant, Margaret Cathcart, who was to have been married to Kerr. Constant efforts are being made, by the gentry of Fermanagh, to obtain a full pardon for Cathcart. During the time of the execution, a policeman fell insensible to the ground.

The last public hanging in Ireland was in 1868 with executions thereafter confined to behind prison walls. For much of the nineteenth century, transportation remained an alternative to hanging for many crimes. Early destinations had been North America and the West Indies. The American War of Independence had brought to an end the transportation to North America and with the jails becoming overcrowded Parliament sanctioned transportation to Australia. *The Queen*, the first Irish convict ship, sailed from Cork in April 1791. The number of transportations gathered pace after the economic downturn which followed the end of the Napoleonic Wars. Looking at the assize court books for County Antrim one can see that there was a large number of larceny offences for which transportation was adjudged appropriate punishment. For example, for the 130 convictions at the Co Antrim assizes in Carrickfergus in 1827, eighty were for grand larceny – that is, theft of goods to the value of more than twelve pence. Of these, forty were sentenced to transportation.

Convict settlements were a feature of Australian society for nearly a century until the transportation system was progressively withdrawn from 1840 onwards. It has been estimated that between 1788 and 1853 about 40,000 Irish criminals were shipped directly from Ireland to Australia. Another 8,000 Irish men and women were sent into penal exile from courts in Scotland and England. In that year, New South Wales was removed from the system. It was followed by Tasmania in 1852 and Western Australia in 1867. The main reason for this was that the Australian colonists came to regard the convict system as a stigma on those who had chosen to emigrate, as well as criticism in both Britain and Australia because of the inevitable brutality of certain aspects of the convict system.

Before the middle of the eighteenth century imprisonment was rarely used as a punishment for felony. For major crimes such as highway robbery, housebreaking, grand larceny and murder, the normal penalty was death; otherwise sentences were short. Prisons were more a method of confinement for those in debt waiting for trial than a place of punishment. Life inside these prisons could be hard according to a police magistrate's report for the Sheriffs' Prison Dublin in 1809. It found the prison:

> in a state of filth and dirt, loathsome to a degree. One cell under the very body of the building, had been converted into a common dirt hole into which all of the dirt of the prison had been put for 6 months. Walls of apartments had not been whitewashed within memory of any confined within, and were covered with vermin. The prison was for debtors only, but the unfortunates had to rent this miserable accommodation from the Keeper at prescribed rates, or from the original tenant at greatly enhanced rates for only a portion of the cell. The magistrates obviously suspected the Keeper of sharing in the profits, but were unable to verify their suspicions. The sewers were all out of order and part of the iron railing to the stairs broken away. The Keeper when spoken to about the dirt said he could not afford to keep it clean as besides the fees he paid the Registrars of the Judges for bringing up prisoners, he had to pay the Sheriffs £100 a year, which, if true, was quite illegal.

On the other hand Mr and Mrs Hall found the jails of Cork city and county, 'models of management, cleanliness and order.' However, they were critical of Irish jails for their 'want of classification' so that 'atrocious criminals and petty offenders are mixed together in a manner sadly prejudicial'. They found this particularly true of Clonmel Jail where:

Gladstone Street, Clonmell.

the prisoners were placed before us in files; among them we saw an elderly
and respectable-looking man striving to hide his face with his hat and step-
ping back to elude observation. We found that he had been confined for
drunkenness, but that the person next to whom he stood was about to be
tried for sheep stealing, and had previously been in custody on suspicion
of murder.

Kohl observed in the mid-1840s, after a visit to the same County Gaol, that for
many prison offered a more luxurious life than they could hope for at home:

> The entire prison is built of iron and stone; and as Paddy's dwelling is usu-
> ally constructed of earth or mud, it may be said, without exaggeration, that
> for the commission of a wicked crime an Irishman is removed from a hole
> to a palace. His diet is also, in general, very much improved; for while he
> remained at home, with unimpeached honour, he had only watery potatoes;
> but as an offender in prison, he receives daily two pounds of bread and an
> allowance of milk along with it. It would, indeed, be difficult to make Paddy
> more uncomfortable in gaol than he is at home.'

In his opinion such a system produced 'a peculiar and numerous class of offenders, who have entirely lost their love of freedom, and who because they live as
well or better in gaol, do not scruple, after being set free, to offend again, and
again to be imprisoned'.

Regular visits from well-meaning worthies were just one of the hardships
faced by prisoners and, in spite of Kohl's opinion that many were better off
inside, it did not stop some from absconding at the first opportunity. According
to the *Waterford News* for 31 October 1851:

> On Sunday morning last, a man of the name of James Regan, who was
> tried at Lismore Quarter Sessions, for stealing apples, the property of Mr.
> Baldwin, and was sentenced to seven years transportation, most unfortu-
> nately made his escape out of the Bridewell. It appears that a house took
> fire in the vicinity of the place, which attracted the notice of the congrega-
> tion that was coming from mass at the time, together with the inhabitants
> of the locality who assembled on the occasion. Ryan [*sic*] thinking this a
> fit opportunity of making his exit, took off his coat and hat, and brought a
> piece of stick with him, worked his body through the chimney, and when
> he came out at the top, he placed his hat and cap on the stick while he
> slipped down to the gutter, and from this he got down by the shoot, land-
> ing safely on the ground. During the great bustle he was not perceived by

the police or military, and had full time to be many miles distant before he was discovered. At length the police casting a vigilant eye around the prison, perceived the coat and hat, and they called out in a stentorian voice, 'go back prisoner, or you will be shot'. There was no reply. Then the police became so provoked and exasperated at the obstinacy and stupidity of the supposed criminal, that they fired at him! But, behold you, instead of killing him, they only perforated his old coat and hat!!!

7

RELIGION

There are few countries in Western Europe where the Church, of various denominations, has had such a profound impact on the lives of local people than in Ireland. In the early nineteenth century the three major denominations – Roman Catholic, Anglican and Presbyterian – between them accounted for all but a very small proportion of the Irish population. In 1861, only 146 people described themselves as being of no religion, or else atheists, freethinkers, deists, materialists, or in some other term implying a rejection of conventional religious belief. Even then, the census commissioners were at pains to point out that of the seventy-two persons who identified themselves as being of 'no religion' seven 'were children under five years of age, and presumed to be unable to answer for themselves'.

Religion was a badge of difference rather than a unifying factor in Ireland throughout the nineteenth century, as James Johnson complained in *A Tour of Ireland* (1844):

> The Jew and Mahamodan do not more cordially despise and detest each other's creeds, than do the Protestant and Catholic sections of the same religion! This sectarian bigotry (for it does not deserve the name of religion) insinuates itself into and mingles with all the transactions of private life. It is carried even to exclusive dealing. The tea of a Protestant grocer would stick in the gorge of a Catholic consumer, and *vise versa*.

Religion was dictated not only by class but by ancestry as Kohl found:

> The three religions of Ireland, the Presbyterian, the Episcopalian, and the Roman Catholic, correspond with the three races which inhabit it – with the descendants of the original Irish, and of the earliest English colonists,

who are all Catholics; with those of the later English immigrants, who are
Protestants; and with the Scottish, who profess Presbyterianism.

From 1537 until 1870, the Church of Ireland was the state church in Ireland. In
order to preserve the English interest in Ireland, nearly all the higher posts in
the Irish Church were filled with Englishmen, often persons who had missed
promotions in England, and the clergy were recruited from among the lesser
Irish gentry. Samuel Hussey in his *The Reminiscences of an Irish Land Agent* (1904)
recalled, 'So far as I can recollect, among all the Irish clergy I have met not one
was an Englishman, though there are plenty of Irish in the English Established
Church.' The Irish gentry who entered the church he conceded:

> whilst, perhaps, richer in proportion than many of the curates and incum-
> bents in England, there are no 'fat' livings, and all are distinctly poorer since
> the Disestablishment. The average in Kerry, and over most of the south of
> Ireland, is a stipend of two hundred pounds a year, which involves reading
> services in two churches each Sunday, and therefore puts the clergyman to
> the expense of keeping a horse and trap.

As members of the established Church they were expected to maintain a certain standing in the local community. John Fitzgibbon commented in 1868:

> The Protestant rector of a parish must support the rank of a gentleman. That
> he shall have a family is not only allowed, but expected; and that he shall
> maintain them with decency in his proper rank is imperative upon him. The
> curates also must keep their place as gentlemen upon stipends which seldom
> exceed the wages now paid to carpenters and bricklayers, and other skilled
> labourers, in Dublin, and other cities in Ireland.

Although it was initially committed to spreading Protestantism to the native
Irish population, its congregations were made up mostly of English and Scottish
settlers and officials. The vast majority of landowners were Anglican, and outside Ulster its membership consisted mostly of people from the professional
classes. Fifty per cent or more of all barristers, solicitors, civil engineers, medical
men, architects and bankers are listed in the 1861 census as members of the
Church of Ireland. Unlike the Church of England, which claimed to represent
the majority of Englishmen, the Church of Ireland embraced only a minority
of the population – no more than 12 per cent according to the census returns
of 1861. 'A Church', Marcus Beresford Archbishop of Armagh and Primate of
Ireland, declared when its critics dismissed it as a minority church:

Archbishop's Palace. (Armagh Public Library)

St Patrick's Catholic Cathedral, Armagh. (PRONI, Allison Collection)

that embraces so large a proportion of the educated classes, which numbers among its members the inheritors of the great historic names of the Country, a majority of the learned professions, and the mercantile classes, and which has implanted the principles of industry, order and loyalty for which the protestant population is so remarkable, cannot be said to have failed in its mission.

It was however notably in decline in many parts of the country. Edward Wakefield, writing of County Waterford in 1812, declared that, 'It is not unusual to see church walls grown green in the inside, and the clergyman dressed in a surplice covered with iron-mould spots, which perhaps had not been washed for twelve moths, delivering a discourse to a congregation composed of from two to six persons'. Nevertheless, those with social ambitions were attracted to the church of the establishment. Mr and Mrs Hall found that:

> At one time many of the principal families in Ulster, particularly in Antrim and Down, were Presbyterians; but their descendants with very few exceptions, conformed to the Established Church; and their example is pretty generally followed by such of the mercantile and manufacturing classes as have attained to that wealth and standing which enable them to associate with the higher ranks.

The Church of Ireland was tasked with civil administration and was therefore responsible for the upkeep of parish schools and roads, for the burial of the destitute, the welfare of foundling or deserted children, and for looking after the poor. This gave the Anglican clergy considerable authority in their parish, and this was reinforced by their close relationship with the local gentry, a fact that contributed to their unpopularity amongst Catholics and dissenters. The imposition of the tithe system to support the Church of Ireland clergy only increased popular hostility towards the local incumbent. The tithe system, which nominally earmarked one-tenth of the produce of the land for the maintenance of the clergy, created a great deal of ill feeling. There was a great deal of opposition to payment in kind which became part of the movement for reform during the 1830s. Farmers who refused to pay their due had their goods seized and sold on. James Hall in his *Tour Through Ireland*, published in 1813, observed:

> In every parish there is a pound-park, to which they take the cows, pigs, calves, and the like, of those who are in arrear for tithes. In eight days after the cattle have been in pound, if the owner do not come and relieve them, by paying the tithe and other expenses, the cow, or whatever it may be, is sold to the highest bidder; and the balance, if any, after paying what had been due, and all expenses, is given to the person to whom the animal, or thing, belonged.

Tithes became increasingly unpopular after Catholic Emancipation was secured. An organised campaign of resistance to collection began in the early 1830s. Spasmodic violence broke out in various parts of Ireland, particularly in

William Gladstone.

Counties Kilkenny, Tipperary and Wexford. In 1839 parliament introduced the Tithe Commutation Act which reduced the amount payable directly by about a quarter and made the remainder payable in rent to landlords. They in turn were to pass payment to the authorities. Tithes were thus effectively added to a tenant's rent payment. This partial relief and elimination of the confrontational collections ended the violent aspect of the campaign against tithes.

It was to mark the beginning of a series of legislative changes that the Church of Ireland was subjected to during the nineteenth century. Most controversial of these was Prime Minister William Gladstone's Irish Church Act of 1869, which dissolved the union between the Churches of England and Ireland and ended the Church of Ireland's position as the established Church. 'So long as that Establishment lives', Gladstone had warned, 'painful and bitter memories of Ascendancy can never be effaced.' The legislation was carried through its various stages in the face of a united and powerful opposition. William Lee, Archdeacon of Dublin, referred scornfully to those politicians who would 'deal with the worship of God as with a question of free trade'. Undeterred, Gladstone successfully guided the legislation through against considerable opposition in both the Lords and the Commons in less than five months, which was described by the *Annual Register*, 1869, as 'the most remarkable legislative achievement of modern times'.

Meanwhile, the Roman Catholic Church remained the overwhelmingly dominant creed in Ireland. In 1861 Catholics made up a minority of the population in four Ulster counties (Antrim, Armagh, Down and Londonderry) as well as in the towns of Belfast and Carrickfergus. In two other Ulster counties, Fermanagh and Tyrone, they accounted for not much more than half the population. Elsewhere in Ireland, Catholics were everywhere a substantial majority, making up 86 per cent of the population in Leinster, and more than 90 per cent in both Munster and Connacht. Dr John Forbes, who toured Ireland in the middle of the nineteenth century commented:

> My experience in Ireland, hitherto, had certainly been almost entirely that of a man travelling in a Catholic country; so small a portion of the whole field of observation did the Protestant element seem to occupy: and … this decided Catholic character assumes even a still more striking aspect when presented in its Sunday dress.

The nineteenth century was a period of progress and reform for the Catholic Church, following the removal of almost all of the legal obstacles imposed on it in the previous century. Significant building work was carried out throughout the century and a new generation of reforming bishops brought their influence to bear on the lower clergy through regular conferences, retreats and visitations. Under Archbishop Cullen who became Ireland's first cardinal in 1866, the Church was brought back into full discipline with Rome. Symbolically, Roman dress became the fashion among the priesthood during the Cullen era. Strong efforts were also made to regulate the behaviour of the wider Catholic community, particularly in regard to the rituals of faith. The restrictions of the previous century had led to a wide variation in religious practice and the merging of popular folk customs with Christian events.

Spring wells were one such phenomenon which came in for clerical opposition. The *Ordnance Survey Memoirs* for the parish of Down, written in 1836, noted that local people were in the habit of coming at certain times of the year to Struell Wells and carrying off portions of the earth and stones as preventatives of disease:

> On St John's Eve (23 July) the people were formerly in the habit of coming to this place in great numbers from all parts of the country for the purpose of performing various penances. The crowds were at sometimes immense. Several heaps of stones were placed in different positions over the ground and the penitents were obliged to walk on their bare knees, first round all these heaps and then up a steep and stony acclivity to a portion of rock which was termed St Patrick's Chair, where a person received them and dismissed them. They then went to the places for bathing … and washed themselves. This practice has been rapidly declining of late years, it having been forbidden by the clergy of the Roman Catholic Church.

It is perhaps not surprising that such a gathering provoked a hostile response from the church for it was the custom for penitents to bathe in the wells at two specially constructed bathhouses. 'Even within the last 5 or 6 years the practice existed to an extent that appears extraordinary,' declares the *Memoirs*:

> and the bathing house…was seen filled by from 30 to 40 people of both sexes in a state of perfect nudity. During the time that these ceremonies were going on, the ground in the neighbourhood used to be covered with tents for the sale of whiskey, and the Sunday after St John's Eve was devoted to all kinds of mirth and festival.

The dedication of Irish Catholics to the Church was remarked upon by numerous travellers. Dr John Forbes visited two Catholic chapels in Limerick, St Michael's and St John's in 1852 both in the morning and afternoon during the time of service. He was impressed by the fervour of the congregation:

> It was a striking sight, and not a little touching, to see those children of poverty at their devotions; kneeling, crouching, many stretched at full length upon the ground, as if dead; others striking their breasts, or holding up

their hands fixedly in the air, or counting their beads; and all uttering their responses in the most earnest tones – all apparently in that profound absorption of the faculties, which indicates utter oblivion of everything external. Many children were present, and exhibited as much fervour of devotion as their seniors. A few of the women had books, more had rosaries, but the majority had neither.

In 1887, Paschel Grousset, an exiled French journalist, noted that the Catholics he met were:

Catholics not so only in name. The greater number follow the services of the Church, observe all the rites, maintain a direct and constant intercourse with priests. The sincerity of their faith is particularly striking, and is not to be found in the same degree even in Italy or in Spain.

This devotion became more marked as the century progressed, as many sought refuge in the Church from the immense cultural, social and economic changes that were taking place around them. This devotion sometimes manifested itself in the sort of phenomenon that took place at the village of Knock, County Mayo, on the evening of 21 August 1879, when a group of men, women, and children witnessed an apparition of the Virgin Mary, Joseph and Saint John the Evangelist at the south gable end of the local small parish church. The site quickly became a place of pilgrimage. On her travels in Ireland, Margaret Dixon McDougall visited Knock and noted:

As I stood looking, the car man came in after tying his horse, and knelt down on the damp earth before the Virgin's shrine and repeated a prayer. He was not ashamed to practice what he believed before the world and in the sight of the sun. When his prayer was over he joined me, and drew my attention to the number of crutches and sticks left behind by those who were benefited. I pointed out to him a very handsome black-thorn stick among the votive offerings, and asked him would it be a sin to steal it, as black-thorns were in demand over the water. He told me if I did that whatever disease was laid down there by the owner of the stick would cleave to me.

Parish priests were held in high regard by the majority of the community; their income and place in society was never in doubt. Religious life in towns, and increasingly in villages and rural areas, was centred around the chapel. Individuals and families depended on the Church for the celebration of the rites of passage such as baptism, marriage and death. Sunday mass and a range of meetings, societies and devotions provided a wide range of opportunities for the cultivation and expression of religious faith and strengthened the links between priest and people. The life of a rural priest was a hard one nevertheless, as Dr John Forbes noted in 1852:

> Generally speaking, the style of living of the rural priests, whether parish priests or curates, is hardly what would be called in England genteel or even comfortable; partly in consequence of their scanty revenues, and partly, perhaps, on account of the comparatively isolated and lower social position they occupy. Unlike the clergy of England, whether Protestant or Catholic, the priests in Ireland are permitted to hold but rare social intercourse with the gentry in their own neighbourhoods – greatly, I should say, to the discredit of the gentry, and greatly to the loss of the community … I own I was surprised to find, in my limited intercourse with the priests of both degrees, how well they preserved the character of gentlemen, both in their manners and external appearance. I found them always well-dressed, very polite, and with the conversation of men who had been well-educated.

The Catholic clergy relied on the contributions of their parishioners for their subsistence. This created a close bond between the clergy and their flock as noted by Alexis de Tocqueville in 1835:

> There is an unbelievable unity between the Irish clergy and the Catholic population. The reason for that is not only that the clergy are paid by the people, but also because all the upper classes are Protestants and enemies. The clergy, rebuffed by high society, has turned all its attention to the lower classes; it has the same instincts, the same interests and the same passions as the people; state of affairs altogether peculiar to Ireland, a point which one should keep well in mind in speaking of the advantages of voluntary remuneration.

For much of the nineteenth century Presbyterian ministers were not so dependent on the generosity of their flock. They had their stipends paid through the *regium donum* – literally 'the King's gift'. The *regium donum* was an annual grant formerly voted by Parliament to augment the stipends of the Presbyterian clergy in Ireland. The grant was then renewed and increased by King William III in 1690 as a reward for the loyalty of Presbyterians during the war in Ireland following the Glorious Revolution. Ironically, this grant to Presbyterian clergy was regarded by some of their congregation with suspicion. James Hall, on his tour though Ireland in 1813, found that:

Presbyterians become more numerous as you advance northward; but, through the increasing numbers of dissenters from them, I am afraid the hook which has caught the clergy, will not retain the people. The truth is, the people already are beginning to be less under their influence, since the Presbyterian clergy, in the north, have been allowed something yearly from government; it having made them, in the opinion of many, less diligent and dependant on the people; who, though not fond of parting with their money, yet like to see their clergy depending on themselves.

It was finally discontinued in 1869 with the act that disestablished the Church of Ireland.

Revd Henry Cooke by Vincent McDonnell.

Presbyterianism came to Ireland from Scotland with the first plantation of Ulster during the early seventeenth century. The Presbyterian population was heavily concentrated in Ulster, where 96 per cent of its members lived. In Counties Antrim and Down, and in Belfast and Carrickfergus, Presbyterians were the largest single religious group. Congregations of Presbyterian settlers were also established during the Cromwellian period at Athlone, Clonmel, Dublin, Limerick and Mullingar. Margaret Dixon McDougall, who toured Ireland in the late nineteenth century, visited Duncairn Presbyterian church and was struck by a singular fact:

> Found myself half an hour too early, so watched the congregation assemble. The Scottish face everywhere, an utter absence of anything like even a modified copy of a Milesian face. Presbyterianism in Ulster must have kept itself severely aloof from the natives; there could have been no proselytizing or there would have been a mixture of faces typical of the absorption of one creed in another.

The Presbyterian had long been an object of suspicion with the authorities. For much of the eighteenth century their freedom of action was severely curtailed by the Penal Laws so that technically it was illegal for Presbyterian ministers to perform marriages of members of their congregation until 1782 and it was not until 1845 that they could legally marry a Presbyterian and a member of the Church of Ireland. It is hardly surprising therefore to find that Presbyterians consistently made up the majority of emigrants from Ulster to Colonial America, while many of those who remained in Ireland became prominent in movements for reform, culminating in the revolt of the United Irishmen in 1798.

This radicalism survived into the early nineteenth century as John Gamble found when he toured the North of Ireland in 1812:

> Presbyterians, I have elsewhere remarked, are enthusiasts in favour of liberty they bow down reluctantly to kings, lords, or bishops, and to get rid of them, particularly the two latter, as much as to better their condition, was probably the reason why so many of them emigrated to America. It is not wonderful, therefore, that almost universally they took part with her in her struggle for freedom, as they would consider it.

By the middle of the nineteenth century the dominant figure in Ulster Presbyterianism, cleric Dr Henry Cooke, played a major role in weaning the Presbyterians of Ulster away from their old alliance with the Liberals and

Catholics against the Anglican Establishment, and substituting a new alliance with the Unionist Episcopalians against the Catholics which became increasingly marked after Gladstone's conversion to Home Rule. This was a major motivation in his relentless opposition to heresy in his Church, leading orthodox Presbyterians against those of a more radical outlook who subscribed to more Liberal Unitarian doctrines led by his rival, Henry Montgomery. In 1829, mainly as a result of his efforts, Presbyterian ministers with Unitarian or Arian views withdrew from the General Synod of Ulster and formed the Remonstrant Synod which was the beginning of what is now known as the Non-Subscribing Presbyterian Church in Ireland. Henry Montgomery, with considerable justification, accused Cooke of uniting Evangelicalism and Orangeism which would become an increasing feature of Presbyterianism as the century progressed.

The failure of the United Irish Rising prompted many Presbyterians to seek solace in the increasingly Evangelical flavour of Protestantism. The Evangelical emphasis on faith, the literal truth of the Bible and personal conversion contrastied with what its supporters saw as the worldliness of the Church of Ireland. James Hall had little taste for the Presbyterian style of sermon and commented sardonically in his *Tour Through Ireland* (1813) of a visit to Coleraine, County Londonderry, 'The people here may be pious and good; but, so far as I can learn, the eternity of hell-torments, the lake that burneth with fire and brimstone, the great and terrible God, the groans of the damned, and the like, are the never-failing topics of their preachers.'

One of the most remarkable events of the nineteenth century was the 1859 revival which swept through most of the towns and villages in Ulster, and in due course brought 100,000 converts into the churches. One of the most interesting aspects of this phenomenon was the almost electric speed with which it spread among female workers in several mills simultaneously. It is reported in the *Banner of Ulster* that on Tuesday 7 June, in one of the departments of a local spinning mill, a number of female staff were suddenly affected:

Within two or three hours on the morning mentioned, nearly twenty of these girls were struck down − each in an instant − at their work; several becoming apparently insensible at once, and others uttering agonising cries for mercy. The scene produced the greatest excitement throughout the entire works, and not a little alarm. The persons prostrated were, however, promptly attended to by the humane manager and by their companies. Cars were provided for those who could not otherwise be removed to their homes, and the rest were assisted out of the premises, and taken to their respective places of abode. Orders were given that the workrooms should be closed for the day; but some additional cases of visitation occurred even as the young women were leaving the place and passing down the stairs. Some of those attacked have not yet been able to return to work.

Many local mill and factory owners were less than happy about this sort of disruption to their businesses. Measures were taken to stop such manifestations with workers being warned that if they dared to attend any revival meetings or were to fall down at their work they would immediately be discharged. According to the *Banner of Ulster*, 'One little boy … was seen pointing out a passage of Scripture to two female workers, when the manager took the Bible from him, locked it up, and in the evening discharged all three'.

The Commissioners of Public Instruction in 1834 recorded a total of only 21,808 persons of other denominations, although this, they noted, excluded a considerable number of Wesleyan Methodists 'who, although attending religious service in other places of worship, consider themselves to be in connection with the Established Church, and wished to be classed as members of that body'. One of the most prominent groups outside the three main denominations was the Religious Society of Friends, also known as 'Quakers' or 'Friends', which originated in the north-west of England during the mid-

Quaker Soup House, Cork. (*Illustrated London News*, 16 January 1847)

seventeenth century. Outside Dublin, the Quakers had settled in a few areas. The initial concentrations were in Ulster at Grange, Richhill, Lurgan and Lisburn; the richer agricultural areas in central Leinster; isolated small urban centres like Wicklow and Carlow; and the major coastal trading cities such as Dublin, Cork, Waterford and Limerick.

By the beginning of the nineteenth century Irish Quakers were highly visible as artisans, shopkeepers, merchants, and professionals. Some Quaker manufacturers became household names, like Jacobs the biscuit-makers and Bewleys who established a chain of cafés in Dublin from 1840. Quaker families were also heavily involved in the linen industry in the North. The Richardson family imposed their Quaker outlook on the village of Bessbrook, providing free medicine and non-sectarian education to its inhabitants. The Quakers also distinguished themselves in charitable work and are warmly remembered for their activities to help the starving and destitute during the Great Famine.

Jews have lived in Ireland since at least the Middle Ages. From the 1820s a new Jewish population appeared, mostly of German and Polish origin, but coming to Ireland via England. They included a high proportion of goldsmiths, silversmiths and watchmakers and merchants. Kohl was struck in the 1840s by how few Jews he encountered when compared with continental Europe:

> It is a fact equally remarkable, and not less strange, that there are no Jews in Ireland; at least there does not exist a single synagogue in the whole of Ireland, not even in Dublin, although it contains 270,000 inhabitants ... In this respect Ireland and Dublin probably stand alone in Europe. In England, and in Scotland also, gipsy's and Jews are every where to be met with. Even in China there are Jews. In Ireland alone there are none. What a short distance we need travel to find out the marvellous!

Their numbers remained small, with only 393 Jews in 1861 and 285 in 1871. From the 1880s their numbers were reinforced from Eastern Europe, mainly because of persecution in Tsarist Russia, and between 1861 and 1901 the population rose from less than 400 to almost 4,000, of which over half was to be found in Dublin. They were a more visible presence as noted by French visitor Madam de Bovet in 1891:

> Most of the rag-dealers being Jews, as is the custom of the children of Israel, they understand their business, and are the only fat and flourishing inhabitants of St Patrick Street. Their crowded shops are the clubs of the place. The purchase of a pair of trousers, a petticoat, or a shirt – which, to judge by the

length of time it takes, seems a most complicated business – is only an excuse
for gossiping, with that wild intemperance, that superabundance of exclama-
tion and expletives that the Irish have in common with southern races.

Another group who fled persecution at home for the relative religious freedom to be found in Ireland were the 'Poor Palatines' as they became known,
due to the fact that they were destitute, left their Rhineland homes for Ireland
during the early eighteenth century. The main settlements were in Counties
Limerick and Kerry. As late as 1840 Mr and Mrs Hall described the Palatines as
superior in character to their neighbours:

> Even now they are a very different in character, and district in habits from the
> people in the country. We visited several of their cottages, or they are better
> pleased to call them 'houses', in the neighbourhood of Adare; and the neat-
> ness, good order, and quality of the furniture – useful and ornamental – too
> surely indicated that we were not in a merely Irish cabin. Huge flitches of
> bacon hung from the rafters; the chairs were in several instances composed
> of walnut tree and oak; massive and heavy, although rudely carved chests
> contained, as we were told, the house linen and woollen, and the wardrobes
> of the inhabitants. The elders of the family preserve, in a great degree, the
> language, customs, and religion of their old country; but the younger mingle
> and marry with their Irish neighbours.

A rigid observation of Sunday was a feature of the north of Ireland that was
remarked on by many visitors. Thackeray commented when travelling through
the north:

> The town of Coleraine, with a number of cabin suburbs belonging to it, lies
> picturesquely grouped on the Bann river: and the whole of the little city was
> echoing with psalms as I walked through it on the Sunday morning. The
> piety of the people seems remarkable; some of the inns even will not receive
> travellers on Sunday; and this is written in an hotel of which every room is
> provided with a Testament, containing an injunction on the part of the land-
> lord to consider this world itself as only a passing abode.

In 1891, French visitor Madam Boret wrote:

> Sunday is no joke in Belfast. As the hotels generally have a public bar, the
> door is locked during the hours of Divine service, and travellers are obliged
> to have it opened for each entry. Needless to say that every kind of spirituous

liquor is freely supplied in the dinning room, or that drunkenness goes on at a great rate in the suburbs all Sunday evening. But the moral discipline of this very religious town forbids all entry into public-houses during service; I say entry, because those who are in can remain behind drawn blinds all the time of mass or sermon. This exterior rigidity of Sunday manners hardly exists to-day save under Protestant auspices.

In the cities, nevertheless, religion did not feature strongly in the lives of many people. According to the Revd W.M. O'Hanlon, Congregationalist minister for the church in Upper Donegall Street, there were parts of Belfast where few Protestant or Roman Catholic Clergy braved the streets unless sent for on special occasions. On one walk through the town he calculated, '307 families who are connected with no denomination of Christians, and never enjoy the ministrations of the Sabbath or the Sanctuary'. Of Beatty's entry and Hamill's-court, in the Millfield area, O'Hanlon found:

> We found the moral and religious condition of the people here quite in keeping, as it generally is everywhere, with their external circumstances. We were given to understand that the face of a Christian instructor is never seen there, nor could we find that the people attend any place of worship on the day of rest. We inquired of a woman, who professes to be a Presbyterian, how long it was since she had been at her Meeting-house or Church, and she replied, it was twelve months. Her plea was the common one – the want of suitable clothes to appear in among respectable people; and I suppose her case might be regarded as a fair sample of the ordinary state of things, in this respect, among all parties in this and similar districts.

This was, he pointed out, 'by no means the worst quarter of the town'.

For many Sunday was just another day to search for work. Kohl, on his way through County Clare in the mid-1840s was:

> grieved as I passed on the Sunday through several towns to see so many poor fellows loitering about, and on the look out for work. They were most of them in their Sunday attire, but with their spades in their hands, and stood grouped about the churches and market-places waiting to be hired to dig potatoes. I was shocked at the sight of such sad and serious multitudes, and all unemployed.

Amongst the larger religious denominations in Ireland differences became more marked as the century progressed, particularly in the north-east of the country and in particular Belfast. By the early years of the nineteenth century Catholics formed about one-sixth of the population of Belfast, the majority of them located in the area close to the chapel in Crooked Lane. Relations between the two communities were already in decline however. One factor was rural migration which from the twenties to the middle of the century was mainly Catholic. By 1850 Catholics formed one third of the population as the town was filled by families fleeing the effect of the Great Famine. As Belfast's population grew, clashes between the different religious groups became an increasingly common feature of life in the town. Sectarian rivalry manifested itself in waves of rioting beginning with a clash on 12 July 1813 and continuing throughout the nineteenth and twentieth centuries. In 1886 the *Belfast News Letter* noted that local women encouraged the men when the stone throwing waned 'and uttered the most desperate threats to the men who desisted'. By the end of this period Home Rule had been grafted on to sectarian animosity. It was the Home Rule issue which would transform Belfast into the citadel of Irish Unionism and bring together even more closely the fortunes of Protestants of all social classes.

Religious rivalries were also a constant problem in many parts of rural Ulster throughout the nineteenth century. It was in the tiny farms of these areas, where the linen industry flourished, that increasing competition for land, once thought uneconomic, resulted in faction fights at local fairs and markets, culminating in the Battle of the Diamond in September 1796 which led to the formation of the Orange Order. The Order was modelled on the Freemasons and their oath went, 'I ... do solemnly swear that I will, to the utmost of my power, support and defend the King and his heirs as long as he or they support the Protestant ascendancy.'

Despite early government attempts to suppress the organisation, it remained the largest Protestant organisation in Ireland with its annual Twelfth of July demonstrations. The symbols of Orangeism were very visible during the month of July. Margaret Dixon McDougall noted on her visit to Clones: 'I was quartered in the most loyal corner of all the loyal places in Clones. Every wall on which my eyes rested proclaimed that fact.' Here were framed all the mysterious symbols of Orangeism, which were very like the mysterious symbols of masonry to Margaret Dixon McDougall's eyes:

There was King William in scarlet, holding out his arm to some one in crimson, who informed the world that 'a bullet from the Irish came that grazed King William's arm'. On the next wall is the battle of the Boyne, with some pithy lines under:

And now the well-contested strand successive columns gain,
While backward James' yielding band is borne across the plain;
In vain the sword that Erin draws and life away doth fling,
O worthy of a better cause and of a nobler king!
But many a gallant spirit there retreats across the plain,
Who, change but kings, would gladly dare that battlefield again.

Religious tensions could arise in the most unlikely places. According to *The Irish Times*, 6 January 1875, the following incident took place at Menlo, a small village on the outskirts of Galway:

As the remains of the late Sir Thomas Blake, of Meale Castle, were being conveyed last evening for interment to the Menlo churchyard, some rumours were afloat on the way that a scene would ensue, and a subsequent portion of the proceedings served to realise their anticipations. The remains were borne to the churchward by the tenantry, but as soon as the cortege reached the gate leading to the enclosure, a proposal was made to carry the remains to a portion of the ground set apart for Roman Catholics. This was forcibly resisted by the Protestants present, and a long and fierce struggle followed. The Rev. Mr O'Sullivan and other Protestant gentlemen were abused, and some of them assaulted. The Protestants were determined that he should be buried with the funeral rites of their Church; but the Catholic tenantry were much more numerous, and showed as much deter-

Funeral procession. (John Barrow, *Tour Round Ireland: Through the Sea-Coast Counties, in the Autumn of 1835*)

A Portadown shopkeeper, 1892. (Sprott Collection, Portadown College)

mination on the other side. All the available constabulary force of the town were turned out to the scene, and it was with difficulty that even this power could preserve order. Finally the remains were interred, and the funeral service got through.

Schools, hospitals, and other charitable institutions, orphan societies, voluntary organisations, even sporting clubs, tended to be organised along denominational lines. John Gamble noted during his visit to Ulster in 1813: 'In Dublin, and many other towns in the South and West, Catholic and Protestant communities were not segregated as they were in Belfast, but they tended to live separate lives.' Kohl noticed:

I was once recommended not to take off my hat so often, as that was only done by the poor Catholics; and in Cork I lodged at an hotel, the landlord of which was a Protestant and a Tory, and received Protestants only as his guests. Another hotel in the city was, in like manner, exclusively frequented by Whigs and Catholics. In many other towns of Ireland these exclusively

Protestant or Catholic hotels are to be found; and I have been told that there are even public conveyances in which Protestants chiefly travel, and others regularly preferred by the Catholics.

Charlotte Elizabeth, who had toured the Manchester estates in Tandragee with land agent Henry John Porter, found that in Portadown she quickly forfeited her hard-earned Protestant reputation in the eyes of the locals simply by taking the wrong coach:

> Two coaches pass from Armagh to Belfast, nearly at the same time; Mr Porter had advised me to take advantage of the first, if possible, lest there might be no vacancies in the other. We learned from our little driver, that one of these was a Protestant coach, and the other a Roman one; and it was evident which way his predilection lay, by his frequent assurance that there was every prospect of the Protestant coach coming up first.

This was not the case, and when Charlotte Elizabeth secured passage on the coach that drew up:

> one of the locals shouted, 'That is the Popish coach; you won't get into Belfast in any time. The Protestant coach is just coming up. Sure you won't go in that!' and finding me resolved, he at last exclaimed, 'Mr. Porter would not go in that coach for ten pounds.' I could not help laughing, although indignant at the untruths so freely told, evidently by an interested individual on the watch to benefit his own establishment; and the sly humour that played on the features of the adverse party, the quiet drollery of both coachman and guard, suppressed by personal respect, as they most courteously answered my inquiries and installed us in the empty vehicle, formed a favourable contrast to the angry professor of orthodoxy. Lord Mandeville's livery on the one hand, and in the other an order to be set down at the Downshire Arms in Belfast, affording a guarantee for our Protestantism; and I was really glad to prove my dislike of such narrowness, real or assumed, by an extra measure of civility and of liberality towards the Popish coach. 'It is not by making their religion a reproach, and a bar to their success in fair trading or honest labour, that we shall detach the people from it: far otherwise.'

8

EDUCATION SYSTEM

Many travellers to Ireland remarked upon the Irish peasantry's love of learning. 'Education', wrote Edward Wakefield in the early nineteenth century:

> is more general among the poorer classes in Ireland than it is among the same description of persons in England. In the former the peasantry are more quick of comprehension than the latter. Labourers in England can plough the land or make a fence in a manner which would astonish the Irish, but they are so boorishly stupid that it is difficult to converse with them and they seldom trouble themselves about anything beyond the precincts of their own parish. But the Irish, with less skill in manual operations, possess more intelligence, they are shrewd by nature, and have a most anxious desire to obtain information.

William Makepeace Thackeray noted the same phenomenon on a visit to Cork:

> I listened to two boys almost in rags: they were lolling over the quay balustrade, and talking about one of the Ptolemys! and talking very well too. One of them had been reading in 'Rollin' and was detailing his information with a great deal of eloquence and fire. Another day, walking in the Mardyke; I followed three boys, not half so well dressed as London errand-boys: one was telling the other about Captain Ross's voyages, and spoke with as much brightness and intelligence as the best-read gentleman's son in England could do. He was as much of a gentleman too, the ragged young student; his manner as good, though perhaps more eager and emphatic; his language was extremely rich, too, and eloquent.

Although the age of the bard had disappeared, a love for story telling underpinned the Irish attitude to learning. Curwen, in his travels through Ireland in the early 1800s, noted:

during the winter it is a general custom for the neighbouring cottiers
to assemble alternately at each other's cabins about the blazing hearth
of wood procured from the bog, and preserved for such occasions. The
females bring their spinning-wheels and stools, while the children and
men complete the semi-circle on the floor; the oldest patriarch then takes
the lead in narration, and is succeeded by his grey-headed juniors in turn.
The 'tale twice told' loses no little of its force, or interest, but is listened
to by all with delight – the tear of sympathy still flows, and the same glow
of admiration, or indignant flame, still paints on the check the feelings of
the heart.

While the Penal Laws were enforced, Irish peasants were forced to depend
upon hedge schools for their elementary education. These were basically a collection of poor students and a teacher holding class in a ditch or hedgerow,
with one of the pupils serving as a look-out for law officers. They were usually
set up by itinerant schoolmasters who were paid according to the size of the
school. As the Penal Laws were relaxed the master was able to make himself and
his pupils a bit more comfortable, settling in the comparative luxury of a sod
hut or an unused barn for his classroom.

Most hedge masters taught the 'threes Rs', but because of the impediments
to Catholic education, few had been to University or even to secondary school.
The quality of teaching varied enormously. In 1821 Bishop Doyle noted that
the masters 'in many instances are extremely ignorant'. On the other hand,
when Tommy Maher, who had for years taught in a mud hut at Goffs Bridge in
County Wexford, transferred his allegiance to the Board of Education in 1815
and became an inspector. He was amazed:

> at the skill of the twelve-year-old boys in reading the new books, and con-
> sidering the possibility that they were reciting from memory, I invited one
> of their number to read me a passage from the Gospel of Saint Matthew.
> Evidently the child misunderstood me. He searched in his satchel until he
> found his tattered book, stood up, and proceeded to read me the account of
> Christ's passion – in Greek.

The best estimates indicate that in the mid-1820s 300,000 to 400,000 Catholic
children were being educated in this way, for the price of a piece of turf –
a remarkable testimony to the peasantry's enthusiasm for schooling. German
traveller Johann Khol visited one of the last of the old hedge schools during his
stay in Ireland in the 1840s:

The schoolhouse was a mud hovel, covered with green sods, without windows or any other comforts. The little pupils, wrapped up as well as their rags would cover them, sat beside the low open door, towards which they were all holding their books in order to obtain a portion of the scanty light it admitted ... The school-house stood close by the roadside, but many of the children resided several miles off, and even the schoolmaster did not live near it. At a certain hour they all met here; and when the day's task is over the boys put their primers in their pockets and scamper off home; whilst the schoolmaster fastens the door as well as he can, puts his turf fees into his bag, takes his stick and trudges off to his remote cottage across the bog.

As the Penal Laws relaxed in the late eighteenth century, a number of religious orders devoted themselves to the education of the Catholic poor. Catherine McAuley opened her first house of the Sisters of Mercy in Baggot Street, Dublin, in 1828. By 1850 there were 3,000 sisters committed to education in several towns. The Brigidine Sisters, the Loreto Sisters, the Irish Sisters of Charity and the Holy Faith Sisters were all devoted to education and these native foundations were assisted by Irish houses of Ursulines, Dominicans and Sisters of St Louis. Edmund Ignatius Rice established the first Irish Christian Brother's school in Carrick-on-Suir in 1816, and by 1867 there were fifty-five Christian Brothers schools across Ireland.

An alternative to hedge schools or those founded by religious orders was provided by various Protestant societies for the conversion of Roman Catholics. One of the best known is the 'Charter School Society', so called from the Charter of George III (6 Feb. 1734) by which the Incorporated Society in Dublin for Promoting English Protestant Schools in Ireland was established. It was specified that 'the children of the Popish and other poor natives' were to be instructed in the English tongue and the formularies of the established Church of Ireland. It aimed to provide a means of educating the children of Catholics 'before the corruptions of popery have taken root in their hearts', and to produce Protestant wives for English settlers who in the past had married Catholics because they had no choice. It was considered essential that the schools be boarding schools so that the children would be removed from the influence of their parents and priests and as a result they were located in the more remote parts of the country.

The Charter greatly aided the society in its fundraising and from 1738 to 1794 it also received £1,000 annually from successive kings. In 1747 the Irish parliament granted the society the proceeds from the licensing duty on hawkers and peddlers, and parliamentary grants began in 1751 and continued until

Connemara tinker. (Samuel G. Bayne, *On An Irish Jaunting-Car Through Donegal and Connemara*, 1902)

1831. Most of the early schools were also endowed by prominent members of the gentry and Church. The schools laid great emphasis on manual labour and, according to the society's records, each school was provided with a sundial and an hourglass to regulate the children's work. The boys were employed chiefly in agricultural work and the girls at housecrafts.

Masters were appointed to the schools with very small salaries which they augmented by selling the produce of the children's labour. A description of the masters by a critic of the schools in 1806 gives an impression of the quality of teaching. Teachers were described as:

> Men of vulgar habits, coarse manners, often ignorant in the extreme of everything but the common rudiments of reading, writing and arithmetic, exhibiting nothing in conduct or example that could raise the minds of the children above the level of that semi-barbarism which has been the character of the lower class of the people of this country.

An Inquiry into the Charter Schools in 1818 found most children half-starved, living on a potato and milk diet:

> In the country parts of Ireland, boys and girls can be fed on such rations, on an average, for 2d per day, or even less. A few acres of potatoes are sufficient for a whole school, and milk well watered, or butter-milk, would supply them

for a mere trifle. A decent dress for Sundays, and not unfrequently without even that, will enable the master to let them go ragged and half naked the rest of the week. If the boys are indulged in idleness, as a bonus for being half fed and half clothed, their education is thereby neglected, and their morals corrupted. If they are treated with severity, to deter them from complaining, they are tempted to run away and become vagabonds.

There were never more than sixty or so Charter Schools in existence at any one time. A series of private and public inquiries, which culminated in the disclosures of the Irish Education Inquiry of 1825, revealed extensive cruelty and neglect, and shortly afterwards state support was withdrawn. There was also a great deal of Catholic opposition to these Charter Schools. This is hardly surprising if we take a look at the books distributed to the schools which bore titles such as *The hazard of being saved in the Church of Rome* and *Discourse against Transubstantiation together with a discourse showing the Protestant way to Heaven*. Parents were also deterred from sending their children by the cost of such an education. An Inquiry into the Charter Schools in 1818 stated:

> I believe two shillings and sixpence per quarter is the lowest price generally demanded and often it is as high as eleven shillings. The lowest of these sums to a poor man, with five or six children who need education, is more than he can spare, and he is, therefore, compelled to let his children grow up uneducated, how much soever he is anxious for it, unless he can find it in another way.

In 1812 commissioners appointed to inquire into the state of the schools and charities of public foundation recommended that, 'no attempt should be made to influence or disturb the peculiar religious tenets of any sect or description of Christians.' The Society for the Education of the Poor in Ireland, better known as the Kildare Place Society, was founded in 1811 and aimed to provide a system of interdenominational education. Its objective was:

> the admission of pupils, uninfluenced by religious distinctions, and the reading of the Bible or Testament, without note or comment, by all the pupils who had attained a suitable proficiency; excluding catechisms and controversial treatises; the Bible or Testament not to be used as a class book from which children should be taught to read or spell.

For a time is had the approval of the Catholic clergy and laymen. Daniel O'Connell was on the society's board of governors. The Catholic clergy became patrons of individual schools, and the clergy gave their cautious sanction to the society's activities. Educationally, the society was a considerable success, publishing the first major series of sequential textbooks in the British Isles, establishing model schools for the training of teachers, and pioneering the creation of an efficient system of school inspection. By 1820 the society was operating 381 schools, enrolling 26,474 pupils.

In 1820 the Kildare Place Society abandoned its neutral stance and began to allocate part of its own income to the schools of various Protestant proselytising societies, such as the London Hibernian Society, the Baptist Society and the Association for Discountenancing Vice. At the same time, Protestant clergy

Daniel O'Connell.

and lay patrons increasingly ignored the society's rules by taking a proactively sectarian approach to scripture readings. O'Connell resigned in 1820 and led an agitation against the society. A petition signed by the leading Catholic bishops led in 1824 to the establishment of another official inquiry into Irish popular education. By 1830 the number of schools had risen to 1,634, but that same year the parliamentary grant was withdrawn and the number of schools quickly declined.

Statutory provision for a system of education in Ireland had existed and had been in operation since the sixteenth century. However, the task of organising and maintaining the parish schools had been assigned to the Anglican clergy who, being usually poor and non-resident, found it impossible to overcome local hostility. An Inquiry in 1818 declared:

> It is painful to be obliged to state, that not withstanding their solemn and deliberate appeal to Almighty God, in their engagement to keep, or cause to be kept, a school in their parish, a very small proportion of the parishes of Ireland have been favoured with this description of schools. Thus generation after generation has been left with a state of gross ignorance.

Instead it was often the local landlord who took an active interest in education. Mr and Mrs Hall commented in the 1840s:

> The principal proprietor of Tandragee is Lord Manderville, who, with his neighbours, Lords Farnham and Roden, Colonel Blacker and the Marquis of Downshire, have contributed largely to the present cheering condition of the county of Armagh. Lord Manderville has established no fewer than sixteen district schools on his estate in this neighbourhood, for the support of which he devotes £1000 per annum, out of an income which is by no means large'.

The ladies of the big house tended to take an active interest in these schools as Sir John Carr found in 1805:

> It was with great pleasure that I visited Bushy Park, the seat of Sir Robert Shaw, Esq – member for the city of Dublin, whose amiable lady and her sister-in-law I found in a school near the mansion, surrounded by sixty girls: the children of the neighbouring peasantry which were instructed in the useful parts of education, are provided with clothes according to their merit, and with food at the expense of Mrs Shaw. Amongst the children there are only three Protestants: to banish ignorance and superstition by useful instruction; to supersede habits of sloth and vice by those of an opposite tendency; to make good members of society and not converts are the cordial object of this enlightened lady.

It was against this background of haphazard education and falling standards of living that the Irish system of National Education was founded in 1831 under the direction of the Chief Secretary, E.G. Stanley. The National Schools which resulted were built with the aid of the Commissioners of National Education and local trustees. The national system of primary education, established in 1831, antedates by almost a full four decades the establishment of a similar system in England. The curriculum was to be secular in content, though provision was made for separate religious instruction at specially stated times. The board gave assistance to local committees in building schools and made a major contribution towards the teachers' salaries. A teacher-training school was established in Dublin and model schools were set up gradually throughout the county.

School buildings sprang up all over the country. Mr and Mrs Hall, who remembered the old school houses as 'for the most part, wretched hovels, in which the boys and girls mixed indiscriminately', were impressed by the transformation brought about by the Board of Education, 'The school-houses, instead of being dark, close, dirty and unwholesome, are neat and commodious buildings, well-ventilated and in all respects healthful.' They were also impressed with the books supplied by the board. These included an English Grammar, arithmetic books for various classes, books on geometry and book keeping, and *An Introduction to the Art of Reading and a Treatise on Mensuration*. German traveller Johann Khol visited an Irish National School in Wexford in the 1840s and was equally impressed:

The one I visited at Wexford, like most of the Irish infant schools, had only been established five years, and contained ninety-one Catholic and thirty Protestant children. The children usually remain until their twelfth year, but the Catholics often send their daughters back again, as they are dissatisfied with the parochial schools which are attended by those of a more advanced age … The system of education at these infant schools is very peculiar, and, indeed extremely poetical. All the instruction is conveyed in verses, which are sung by the little pupils, and, whenever it is possible, accompanied with a pantomimic acting of the subject. Almost every general movement made by the children is attended with singing. For instance, as they come into the schoolroom they sing the following verse:

We'll go to our places, and make no wry faces,
And say all our lessons distinctly and slow;
For if we don't do it, our mistress will know it,
And into the corner we surely shall go.

As well as receiving an education, girls were taught needlework and the National Education Board encouraged the teaching of agriculture and gardening to boys and girls. The priorities of the Commissioners of National Education are indicated in a set of instructions given to inspectors in 1836:

> He [the inspector] will ascertain the advancement of education among the children, noting the proportion of children who can read fluently; what progress they have made in writing and arithmetic; whether any be taught geography, grammar, book-keeping and mensuration; whether girls be taught sewing or knitting.

The main criticism of the new system came from the churches. The Established Church remained suspicious of these attempts to remove their influence over the education system. In 1839 the Church Education Society was established. Its declared object was to maintain an independent system of schools conducted under the auspices of the Established Church. By 1850 it had 1,800 schools affiliated to it but by the 1870s the expense of maintaining the society drove it into the state system. For a short time in the 1830s the Presbyterian Synod of Ulster also refused to have anything to do with the Education Board. Presbyterians were concerned at the restrictions placed on the use of the Bible and the limited rights of ministers of denominations different from that of the majority of the pupils. Gradually the Board agreed to compromise on the points at issue and by the middle of the Victorian period Presbyterians were receiving grant aid for what was in fact virtually a self-contained system of denominational schools.

Ironically, the Roman Catholic clergy remained suspicious of what they continued to see as a proselytising organisation. The system at first enjoyed the support of the majority of bishops. Opposition soon emerged among a minority, most prominent of whom was Dr McHale, Bishop of Tuam. He believed that the scheme was anti-Catholic and anti-national and argued that education for Irish Catholics should be characteristically Irish and exclusively Catholic. A papal decision in 1841 allowed each bishop to decide whether the schools in his diocese might participate in the National School system.

The attitudes of the Churches eventually led, in practice, to denominational schools under the control of clerical managers from the different religious bodies. In Catholic schools the manager was almost always the parish priest, and in Protestant schools the Rector, Minister, or landlord. He was charged with the daily oversight of the school: he had the right to appoint and dismiss teachers who were to be hired from model or training schools established by the board; he chose which of the several approved sets of textbooks the school would use, and, within broad limits, arranged the school's timetable.

Although by the end of the nineteenth century free elementary schooling was provided for all children, the numbers attending schools in many areas was sparse. Dr John Forbes found in 1853 that attendance at school varied from place to place. At Kenmare, although there were fifty-four boys on the books, only twenty-seven were present on the day he paid his visit. He was told that numbers had dropped because of recent emigration and due to the demands of the present harvest season. Although Acts of 1876 and 1880 prohibited the employment of children under ten years old and children up to thirteen were required to attend school, the Reports of the Commission for Education make it clear that many children made only infrequent attendance at school. In his general report into the Armagh Circuit in 1903 Mr Murphy commented that:

> The character of the attendance remains practically unchanged. The same causes are at work in town and in country and the same unsatisfactory results are noticeable. In rural districts the pupils attend for the most part very irregularly. This is due to the demand for child labour, and partly to a seeming inability on the part of parents to appreciate the injustice they do to their children, when they keep them from school without sufficient reason.

The Mudlark. (Henry Mayhews, *London Labour and the London Poor*)

According to evidence given to the Powis Commission of 1868–70 only 33.5 per cent of pupils made an annual attendance of 100 days, and from 50 per cent to 65 per cent in some counties were found unable to read or write. These and other considerations led to the system of payment by results from 1872. Every pupil was examined in reading, writing and arithmetic. Those in third standard were examined in grammar and geography as well. In fourth and higher standards, pupils faced tests in agriculture, and girls in second and all higher standards were examined in needlework. To be eligible for examination a pupil had to have made one hundred attendances during the year. The inspector examined each pupil and awarded a mark: number 1 was a pass and 0 meant failure. The Education Office then worked out from these marks the amount of the payments to be made.

Although there was some regional variation, overall levels of illiteracy fell rapidly, from 53 per cent in 1841 to 18 per cent in 1891. A.M. Sullivan noted the quiet revolution brought about by the National Schools:

> The average standard of proficiency attained, especially in rural districts, is even still very low, owing to the short and broken periods for which children are allowed to attend school rather than help to earn for home by work in the fields. But, slight as the actual achievement may be in a strictly educational point of view, socially and politically considered, nothing short of a revolution has been effected. There is now scarcely a farm-house or working-man's home in all the land in which the boy or girl of fifteen, or the young man or woman of twenty-five, cannot read the newspaper for 'the old people', and transact their correspondence. Our amusing friend the parish letter-writer has almost disappeared. His occupation is gone.

Increased literacy had a profound impact on the spread of news within a district as noted by A. M. Sullivan in *New Ireland* (1877):

> For public news the peasant no longer relies on the Sunday gossip after mass. For political views he is no longer absolutely dependent on the advice and guidance of Father Tom. He may never find counsellor more devoted and faithful; the political course he may now follow may be more rash or more profitable, more wise or more wrong; but for good or ill it will be his own. He will still, indeed, trust largely to those whom he judges worthy of his confidence, and largely follow their lead; but not in the same way as of yore.

Contemporaries noted that most children left school with the ability to read a newspaper even if 'with difficulty'. The letters from emigrants, the signatures on marriage registers replacing the earlier 'X' and the increase in the number of threatening notices and letters issued during the Land War of 1879-81 were some indications that the National Schools had played a major role in the advancement of literacy in Ireland.

The success of local schools was trumpeted in local newspapers. Readers of the *Belfast News Letter* on Friday 20 August 1858, were informed that:

The annual examination of Anahilt National School, near Hillsborough, was held on Friday, the 6th instant, in presence of the patron, the Rev. Thomas Greer, the committee, and a large number of respectable teachers and visitors. The examination lasted from half-past eleven A.M. till half-past four P.M. The prompt and correct answers of the pupils in the various classes delighted all present, and though time did not permit the examiners to test the capability of the children, ample opportunity was afforded to convince all present of the great excellence of this institution.

Coulter noted that in the West of Ireland where the National Education system took longer to establish itself, emigration provided an important stimulus to its development:

The people are most anxious to have their children educated. The necessity and importance of this has been brought home forcibly to their minds by the letters constantly received from young persons who have emigrated to America. Those who went out ignorant, write home saying that want of education has prevented them succeeding like others in the New World; and those who were fortunate enough to have received a good education before they emigrated, attribute to that fact the success which has attended their exertions among the 'Go-a-head' Yankee people.

There remained an underclass however who never saw the inside of a National School. Vagrant children remained a feature of city life in nineteenth-century Ireland. According to the report of the Inter-Departmental Committee of the Employment of Children during School Age, published in 1902, there were in Dublin 433 boys under sixteen selling chiefly newspapers, and 144 girls selling newspapers, fruit or fish. In Belfast there were 1,240 boys and 45 girls and in Cork, boys only numbering 114. Police returns showed that as a rule these children's lot was a wretched one. The principal dangers were later hours in the street, truancy, insufficient clothing, and entering licensed premises to sell their goods. They were guilty of obstructing, annoying, importuning passengers, begging, fighting with other children, playing football or games in the street, using bad language and smoking.

Ragged schools aimed to tackle this problem. They were non-residential, providing a meal and a few hours education each day for vagrant children. In 1853 there were nine ragged schools in Dublin attended by about 700 children of whom about two-thirds 'were probably thieves' according to evidence given to a parliamentary committee. In 1856 the ragged schools were condemned as centres of proselytism by Catholic Archbishop Cullen.

Ragged school.

Madame de Bovet, who visited the Ragged School in Coombe Street
Dublin opened by the evangelical Irish Church Missions, deplored the
attempts to proselytise:

> It does not really make much difference whether the ragged urchins, who are
> educated at the Coombe Street school, go to mass or to church, but it does
> matter a good deal that children, who might receive a good education, are
> allowed to play in the gutter because their parents refuse to have them taught
> to deny their national faith.

She was nevertheless impressed by the standard of education:

> Apart from this, the organization of the Ragged Schools is worthy of all
> praise. That of the Liberties receives 60 boys as boarders, and more than
> 180 children of both sexes join the classes; another house at Kingstown,
> called The Birdsnest, takes in 300, and connected with it is a kind of crèche,

where 100 little children are taken care of during the day. This class of school is justified by its name. It is a good work educating these little ragged children. The boarders are clothed at the expense of the house, in a blue woollen sailor's jersey, trousers of coarse grey cloth, with stout shoes, and a Scotch cap. Children of drunkards, for the most part, they have the bleached and faded look of the Parisian street boy, though with a less evil countenance, and more robust body. Some of them belong to families of respectable workmen, who rarely get drunk except on Saturday night. Their mother is dead, and they are placed here because there is no one at home to look after them.

For much of the nineteenth century there was no state system of secondary education and what was available was provided by a small number of voluntary schools. When the national system of education was introduced in 1831, many schools which had provided intermediate education ceased to do so because the new Board of Education would only support primary education. In 1837 the Wyse Committee recommended the provision of a centrally funded non-denominational system of intermediate education but until the passage of the 1878 Intermediate Education Act, second-level education was available only in the Protestant diocesan, Royal and Erasmus Smith Schools.

In 1570 an Act of Parliament authorised the establishment of a free grammar school in the principal town of every diocese in Ireland. Little came of this initiative and, by 1791, only eighteen of the thirty-four Protestant dioceses had fulfilled the legislative requirement. Their impact was insignificant for they had in all but 324 pupils enrolled. By 1831 only twelve schools were operating but despite this, the system lingered until 1872. A second phase of secondary school planning was made possible by the Stuart Plantations in Ulster at the beginning of the seventeenth century. As early as 1608, James I decreed that at least one free grammar school should be established in each of the six confiscated Ulster counties. The objectives were: 'To stir up and recall the province of Ulster from superstition, rebellion, calamity and poverty to the true religion of Christ, and to obedience, strength and prosperity'. However, only seven were established at Armagh, Enniskillen, Cavan, Dungannon, Raphoe, Bonagher and Carysfort.

A number of Catholic grammar and diocesan schools were established during the nineteenth century. The *Catholic Directory*, published in 1865, listed sixty intermediate schools, which did not include the fifty-five Christian Brother Schools which were by then in existence and in the higher classes of which there were some intermediate studies. The only counties which had no intermediate schools listed were Tyrone, Fermanagh, Leitrim and Wicklow. These schools were to the Catholic middle class what, for example, the Belfast Academical Institution (opened in 1814) was to the Presbyterian middle class or a public school like St Columba's was to the Church of Ireland middle class.

The Intermediate Education Act (1878) funded secondary education on a payment-by-results basis. This provided serious funding for secondary education and made it more widely available. To avoid accusations that it was bolstering denominational education, the government proposed to indirectly aid schools by conducting annual examinations, rewarding successful candidates with scholarships and certificates and by paying results-based fees to school managers. It marked a great advance in the provision of education generally, particularly for girls. Students could sit any number of subjects but they had to include two of the following: Latin, Greek, English, mathematics and modern languages. The marks allocated to subjects varied. Latin, Greek, English and mathematics were worth 1,200 marks; German and French 700, Celtic (i.e. Irish) 600. Valuable exhibitions (i.e. scholarships) were awarded on a candidate's aggregate marks. Girls' schools competed on an equal basis, and the curriculum in girls' schools changed dramatically as a result. Examinations were held at three levels; junior, middle and senior (and at preparatory level from 1890). Between 1881 and 1911 the number of intermediate schools rose only slightly from 488 to 489 but the number of pupils doubled from 20,000 to 40,000, figures which presented but a tiny fraction of the school-age population.

There was also the fee-paying second-level or intermediate sector, consisting of privately-owned schools and colleges catering almost exclusively for the middle class. As for the curriculum of middle-class schools, there were differences between schools charging a pound a year and those charging four guineas. At the lower end, there was an emphasis on clerical and commercial skills, while the more expensive offered a classical education to boys or a range of accomplishments to girls. Newspaper advertisements provided details of individual schools such as the following which appeared in the *Irish Times*, 12 October 1860:

WOODVIEW SCHOOL, MERRION AVENUE,
BLACKROCK, DUBLIN
RE-OPENED ON THE 1st OF AUGUST
H. T. Humphreys receives as Boarders a limited number of young Gentlemen,
to whose mental and moral culture he pays every attention.

The course of instruction, includes Classics, Science, Modern Languages, and Drawing; and preparation as may be desired, for Commercial pursuits, or for Collegiate or Competitive Examinations.

Scriptural Education is attended to, and the pupils have access to a good library, and to extensive collections in Natural History.

The Playground is large.

Day Pupils are also received.

Exceptional references given and required.

All of these schools were owned by educational entrepreneurs seeking to make a profit by catering for the needs of the middles class. Many of them were extremely short-lived; none of them were accountable except to the parents of their students.

Trinity College, Dublin was founded in 1592 and was the centre of the Protestant Ascendancy, where graduates were required to subscribe to the Oath of Supremacy and Roman Catholics were unable to take degrees until after 1793. Despite the abolition of the Penal Laws, as long as Episcopalian Protestants had the exclusive control of Trinity, neither Catholics nor Protestant Dissenters felt they were receiving equality of treatment in matters of higher education. It was not until 1873 that all religious tests were abolished but it remained a bastion of the Protestant ascendancy as noted by Madam Bovet in the 1890s:

> This university was destined for Protestants only. Catholic students were admitted in 1792, but remained excluded from all privileges of competition. It was not until 1873 that religious distinctions were entirely abolished. They are very low in profiting by this liberal measure if we can believe the last list of undergraduates, which has 771 members of the Episcopalian Church (which are improperly called Anglicans), 80 Presbyterians, 64 Protestants of different sects, and only 81 Roman Catholics.

In 1845 Prime Minister Robert Peel introduced a bill into parliament proposing the establishment of the Queen's Colleges in Belfast, Cork and Galway which were to be strictly undenominational. 'In founding these Colleges', Sir Robert Peel declared in 1845:

> We shall promote social concord between the youth of different religious persuasions, who, hitherto too much estranged by religious differences,

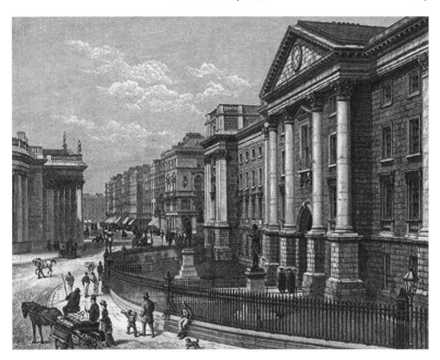

Trinity College and the Bank of Ireland.

will acquire new methods of creating and interchanging mutual esteem. I sincerely believe that, as well as receiving temporal advantages, so far from preventing any advantages with respect to Christianity, the more successfully will you labour to make men good Christians the more they are imbued with that great principle of our faith – a principle which, I grieve to say, many individuals are too apt to forget – the principle, I mean, of reciprocal charity.

Despite opposition from Daniel O'Connell and many Catholic bishops, the colleges were opened in 1848. Papal rescripts condemned the colleges and this contributed to the relative lack of success of the colleges in Cork and Galway. The Presbyterians made the most of the opportunity provided by the establishment of the Queen's College in Belfast.

A Catholic University was established in Dublin, with John Henry Newman installed as rector in 1854. Without a government charter its degrees were without legal recognition, and without state endowment it faced financial difficulties. In the first twenty-five years of its existence from 1854 to 1870 (after which the Catholic University became UCD, administered by the Jesuits) the average yearly intake of students was about twenty-five. The Medical School

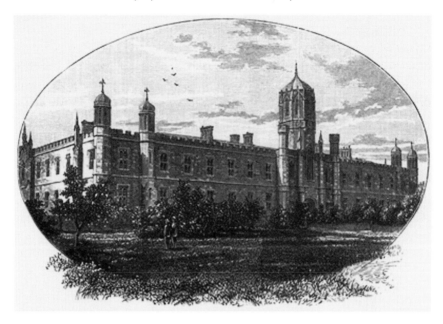

Queen's College, Galway. (Richard Lovett, *Irish Pictures Drawn with Pen and Pencil*, 1888)

which opened in Cecilia Street in 1855 was the Catholic University's great success story. Its examinations were recognised by the Royal College of Surgeons in Ireland and links with the Mater and St Vincent's Hospitals ensured the career prospects of its students.

Women's access to secondary- and third-level education made rather slower progress. As the nineteenth century progressed middle-class women were demanding greater educational opportunities which would enable them to engage in more suitable employment. The establishment of the Ladies' Collegiate School (later Victoria College) in Belfast in 1859 and the Queen's Institute (1861) and Alexandra College (1866) both in Dublin saw an improvement in the educational opportunities for middle-class girls. Leading campaigner for women's educational rights, Isabella Tod summed up the prevailing attitude amongst many middle-class families to their daughters in her pamphlet *On the Education of Girls of the Middle-Classes*, published in 1874, when she declared that middle-class parents, looked forward to:

> all their daughters marrying, to all these marriages being satisfactory, and to the husbands being always able and willing to take the active management of everything …We shall not stop to discuss whether such a state of things is ever desirable. It is sufficient to point out that it does not and cannot exist.

The Royal University of Ireland Act (1879) finally allowed females to take university degrees on the same basis as males. Catholic girls' schools were slower than Protestant girls' schools in doing so but, despite the opposition of senior Catholic leaders, the more progressive religious orders gradually began to enter their female students for the university examinations. Although Trinity College Dublin and the Queen's Colleges (Belfast, Cork, and Galway) remained male bastions, greater opportunities for women in education would ensure that they would play an increasingly important role in the political, cultural and social life of Ireland in the twentieth century.

9

MIGRATION

The Irish were by far the most important migrant group in Britain during the nineteenth century. They made their way to London and to all of the growing industrial towns of the Midlands, the north of England, and the central lowlands of Scotland. Victorian writers associated them with poverty, crime, drunkenness and Catholicism, which helped create the stereotype of the stage Irishman. Thomas Carlyle wrote in *Chartism* in 1840:

> England is guilty towards Ireland; and reaps at last, in full measure, the fruit of fifteen generations of wrong-doing … Crowds of miserable Irish darken our towns … The uncivilised Irishman, not by his strength, but by the opposite of strength, drives out the Saxon native, takes possession in his room. There abides he, in his squalor and unreason, in his falsity and drunken violence, as the ready-made nucleus of degradation and disorder.

However, many prospered in their adoptive country and some, like Oscar Wilde, George Bernard Shaw and W.B. Yeats, scaled the heights of English society.

The emergence of the northern towns as great commercial and industrial centres during the eighteenth century encouraged an influx of Irish settlers. The Irish flocked to Britain during the harvesting period where they followed the harvests round – haymaking in June, turnip-hoeing in July, corn-harvesting in August, hop-picking or fruit-picking in September. The Irish reaper was already a familiar figure in the summer landscape of eighteenth-century England, and by about 1834 it seems from the poor inquiry's parish survey that some forty thousand reapers were migrating annually to Britain. Politician William Cobbett described these seasonal workers as 'squalid creatures … with rags hardly sufficient to hide the nakedness of their bodies'. Those left behind fared little better. A reporter of the *Illustrated*

Seasonal labour force. (*Illustrated London News*)

London News noted the number of beggar women and children in the Irish countryside:

> Where is the husband of that wretched, houseless wanderer from door to door – the father of those 'young barbarians' – where is he? He is in England, reaping and mowing to earn you seven times the value of his little patch of ground that he may keep the hovel of a homestead which is upon it over his family during the hard winter. This must be given up, if whilst away his wife and children cannot get enough to support life, and should present themselves at the gates of the union workhouse. Not a penny of outdoor relief!

The passenger steamers from Ireland were packed between June and October with those seeking work in England and Scotland. Upon leaving Ireland from Londonderry harbour in the 1830s, Charlotte Elizabeth observed:

> A little beyond, we overtook and passed the *St. Columb*, a small steamer bound for Glasgow, so densely crowded with passengers that her bulwarks were fringed by their legs hanging over the sides. These were all poor Irishmen going to seek a precarious employment in the harvest fields, to earn the rent of their miserable cabin, and the dues of their grasping priest.

Connaught Cabin. (Richard Lovett, 1888)

What a monstrous anomaly, that the labouring class of Ireland should thus
be compelled to migrate for a few weeks' employ while her rich bog-lands
are unreclaimed, her fine soil half cultivated, and her abundant mines almost
altogether unworked! Certainly the spirit of blindness is poured out upon
our rulers; and is leading all classes equally or at least similarly astray.

Seasonal migrants were a regular feature of Irish towns and countryside as they
trudged their way to and from the ports. While staying in Edgeworthtown,
German visitor Kohl noted:

Numerous parties of poor Irish reapers and labourers passed through
Edgeworthtown during my sojourn there, and excited compassion by their
miserable appearance. On my way from Dublin I had already met with vast
swarms of them, who all complained of the little they had earned in England.

They were mostly of that class of labourers who wander every year chiefly from the western parts of Ireland, and principally from Connaught, in order to assist the rich English farmers in their harvest. The last year's harvest was very good, but there were so many unemployed hands to be hired at low wages in England, that the Irish emigrants found themselves badly off. Hungry and in rags, they crossed over to England; and in the very same plight they came back, since they had scarcely earned enough to pay the expenses of the journey.

This seasonal migration became a torrent as the potato crop failed over the whole country in 1846 and that failure was repeated in successive years. Many starving and destitute people fled to the industrial towns on the British mainland. Liverpool was the first city to be invaded. At the beginning of 1847 *The Times* warned that 'the anticipated invasion of Irish pauperism had commenced, 15,000 have already, within the last three months, landed in Liverpool and block up her thoroughfare with masses of misery'. By June, it was estimated that 300,000 destitute Irish people had landed in the town. The *Times* predicted that 'in a few years more a Celtic Irishman will be as rare in Connemara as is the Red Indian on the shores of Manhattan'.

In spite of their rural background, the vast majority of these Irish migrants settled in towns. In both 1851 and 1861 at least thirty-one towns in England and Wales had a recorded Irish-born population of over 1,000. Some of the towns are not normally associated with an Irish presence: Bath, Colchester, Derby, Newport, Plymouth, Portsmouth and Southampton. By 1852, 22 per cent of Liverpool's population and 13 per cent of Manchester's was Irish-

Destitution in Ireland. (*Pictorial Times*, 22 August 1846)

born. The largest settlement occurred in London which according to the 1851 census was home to 108,548 Irish-born settlers. Today, more than 150 years after the Famine, the districts settled at that time are still identified as Irish: Hammersmith, Camden Town, Paddington and Islington.

Many Irish settled in London having worked on the land or the railways before becoming highly visible on the streets of the capital. Henry Mayhew noted in the early 1850s:

> These men, when unable to obtain employment, without scruple became street-sellers. Not only did the adults resort to street-traffic, generally in its simplest forms, such as hawking fruit, but the children, by whom they were accompanied from Ireland, in great numbers, were put into the trade, and if two or three children earned 2d a day each, and their parents 5d or 6d each, or even 4d, the subsistence of the family was better than they could obtain in the midst of the miseries of the southern and western part of the Sister Isle.

The Irish were often accused of working for lower rates of pay and thereby depressing wage levels. They were seen as strike-breakers who would gladly work for lower wages. This often led to violent reprisals. In 1826 violence erupted at the Bute Ironworks in the Rhymney Valley, South Wales, when the news spread that cheap gangs of Irish labour were being employed to build new blast furnaces. This anti-Irish violence was a regular feature of industrial relations in Wales for much of the nineteenth century and intensified during the 1860s in response to Fenian terrorist activity in Britain. The industrial-ist George Clark summed up the views of many when he said of his Irish employees at the Dowlais ironworks: 'I believe they are one and all Fenian sympathisers, and I daresay they all subscribe'.

Violence usually took the form of attacks on Irish houses: damaging windows, doors and door-frames. A policeman giving evidence against the rioters in Ebbw Vale in 1879 described the extent of the damage in the Irish district of Newtown:

> I went to Newtown after a time and found houses broken down, but the mob had dispersed. The windows in Crooked Row in which the Irish live were all broken in, frames and all. I visited several of the cottages and saw stones, bricks and parts of the window frames scattered about the floors.

During periods when migration was high, local authorities were faced with the problem of starving and destitute Irish roaming the countryside in search of work. According to the *Doncaster Chronicle* for August 1840:

The influx of Irish reapers into the town of Doncaster during the past week or ten days has been immense, far exceeding that of any other year; and if we are to judge from the numbers who have passed through this town, we should say there is much larger importation than the harvest field will be able to find work for. The town council, in order to relieve those who are really destitute, have granted an allowance of bread to such of them as are considered worthy objects. Within the last ten days nearly 600 of these poor creatures have received relief in Doncaster. The allowance is one pound of bread at night, and half a pound in the morning. In addition to this they are accommodated with a lodging in the rubbing stable adjoining the race course, the floor of which has been covered with clean straw for their reception.

Most local authorities were not so sympathetic and sent back to Ireland families who had fallen on hard times. Long-term residency cut little ice; Irish newspapers are littered with heart-rending stories of destitute families bundled back to Ireland by local authorities in England and Scotland. The *Irish Times* for 4 January 1860 reported:

Sarah Miller, fifty years of age, a native of Belfast, was sent here by the authorities of Newcastle-on-Tyne. She was thirty years in England and Scotland. She was sent to the Union Workhouse, after receiving the necessary attention. Mary Hopkins, twenty-three years of age, and her infant child, were sent here by the authorities of Newcastle-on-Tyne. The poor woman is a native of Mayo, and has been twelve years in England. They were put to lodgings for one night, and then sent to the workhouse, where they remained for five nights. Captain McBride kept them at lodgings for ten nights, and then sent them to Sligo, on the way to where the woman belongs. On the 14th December, Patrick Conway, a poor cripple, was landed from the Glasgow steamer, without money or friends. Captain McBride gave him refreshment, and sent him to the Union Hospital, and when he recovers will send him home to Newry.

Victorian writers frequently portrayed the Irish as living in ghettos, known as 'Little Irelands' which became a nucleus of disease, poverty, alcoholism and crime. Friedrich Engels, in his depiction of Irish immigrants living in the slums of Manchester, helped shape this image:

Here lie two groups of about two hundred cottages, most of which are built on the back-to-back principle. Some four thousand people, mostly Irish, inhabit this slum … The creatures who inhabit these dwellings and even their

dark, wet cellars, and who live confined amidst all this filth and foul air –
which cannot be dissipated because of the surrounding lofty buildings – must
surely have sunk to the lowest level of humanity.

In reality, the Irish in Britain were a diverse group and a significant minority of
them were middle-class people who became more easily absorbed into British
society. In cities such as Bristol there was no Irish quarter and the Irish were
well distributed throughout the city and spanned the whole range of social
groups. In Liverpool, although Exchange, Vauxhall and Scotland Wards were
recognised as Irish districts, they rarely contained more than 50 per cent of
Irish population. Even within Irish communities, there was considerable diver-
sity; both Connaught men and Orangemen from Ulster were looked down
upon by their fellow countrymen and religious differences were a frequent
source of conflict between Irishmen in Britain.

Unfortunately, census records do not distinguish Irish immigrants by
religion and Protestant numbers can only be calculated, where possible, by
subtracting the number of Catholics from figures for the Irish as a whole.
The census of Glasgow in 1831 made by James Cleland, for example, revealed
35,554 Irish out of a total population of 202,426, but only 19,333 were listed
as Catholics. It has nevertheless been estimated that a quarter of Irish immigrants to Scotland during the nineteenth century were Protestant. The first

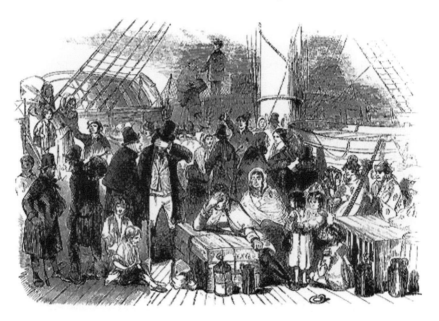

Irish emigrants on the Mersey. (*Illustrated London News*, 6 June 1846)

Orange Lodge set up in Scotland was in the weaving town of Maybole about 1800. By 1835 twelve lodges had been established in Glasgow. By the 1850s Ulster Protestants established specifically Protestant areas such as Govan where they would later become closely identified with Rangers Football Club. Meanwhile, clubs like Celtic and Hibernian maintained close links with the Irish Catholic community in Glasgow and Edinburgh. Until well into the twentieth century matches between the Glasgow rivals would often explode into sectarian violence.

The influx of Irish immigrants ensured that, by the mid-Victorian period, Roman Catholicism was the growing denomination in Britain. From time to time rabid anti-Catholicism exploded into violence. The Stockport Riots of 1852 were partly prompted by the re-establishment from Rome of the Catholic Hierarchy in Britain in 1850. The government reacted by passing the Ecclesiastical Titles Bill which forbade the carrying of Catholic insignia and banners in public places. The Irish in Stockport had risen from 300 at the beginning of the century to over 8,000 by 1852. Their annual procession in June 1852 came only days after the Royal Proclamation of the Ecclesiastical Titles Bill. The procession passed off peacefully but on the following day trouble broke out between rival parties. The rioting lasted spasmodically for three days before it was finally put down by the combined efforts of the police and hundreds of special constables. Sixty-seven people were seriously wounded; one was killed and some died later of wounds. Many Irish families fled to the surrounding countryside.

Throughout the late 1860s the Irish Protestant polemicist William Murphy staged a series of anti-Catholic meetings in English towns. During a meeting in Birmingham in June 1867 he told a gathering of 3,000 people that the Pope was a 'rag and bone picker'. The meeting was attacked by a number of Irish labourers and serious rioting followed, the unrest lasting for several days. Similar outbreaks of violence occurred throughout the winter of 1867 as Murphy travelled around the Midlands, speaking at Stafford, Walsall and other small towns. Similar events took place the following year and in May 1868 a Protestant mob ransacked the Irish sectors of Ashton-under-Lyme, demolishing two chapels, a school and over 100 houses and shops.

This sequence of events was brought to an end in Whitehaven in April 1871. Murphy was scheduled to give a series of lectures but in a pre-emptive strike, between 200 and 300 Irish miners from the nearby pit village of Cleator Moor invaded the town, trapped Murphy in the Oddfellows' Hall and threw him down the stairs. Murphy died a year later but his death was attributed to the injuries he had received in Whitehaven. The death of 'Martyr Murphy' resulted in a resurgence of Orangeism in Cumberland and the north-east of

England. The 1870s and 1880s witnessed numerous outbreaks of street disorder, especially on the 'Glorious Twelfth' of July when Orangemen celebrated the Williamite victory at the battle of the Boyne.

For much of the eighteenth and nineteenth centuries it seemed as if the most energetic part of the Irish population had either left or was about to leave the country. A French visitor to Ireland in the 1880s commented:

> The first thing which attracts the eye in villages and boroughs is a large showy placard representing a ship in full sail, with the following words in large capitals, 'Emigration! Free passage to Canada, Australia, New Zealand! Free passage and a premium to emigrants for Queensland!' Technical particulars follow; the agents' addresses, the names of the outward-bound ships, &c. These placards are everywhere. At each turning, on every wall they stare you in the face, and fascinate the starving man. Numerous and powerful emigration companies paid by colonies where hands are wanting, patronized by all that is influential in the kingdom, work unremittingly in recruiting that army of despair for a voluntary transportation. And thus a continuous stream of Irishmen is ebbing out through all the ports of the country.

In the course of the eighteenth century many of the Presbyterians of the North, irritated by the Test Act and suffering from restrictions on the woollen trade or periodical depressions in the linen industry, emigrated to the English Colonies in America. There was always a steady trickle of Catholic Irish who joined the English Army or Navy and a regular exodus of labourers into England, and this became a mass exodus during the decade during and after the Great Famine when more than 2 million people were to emigrate: more than in the preceding two and a half centuries.

Nineteenth-century emigrants, especially after 1845, were for the most part Catholic. They came mostly from the poorest part of the country – the west – and their emigration was caused by the harsh economic conditions. These emigrants settled to a large extent in the eastern cities of America and the number who took up farming was small in proportion to German and Scandinavian emigrants. The *Irish News* (New York) advised Irishmen to go west, where the poorest emigrant could aquire 40 or 80 acres, pay for it in labour and become independent. However, it advised Irishmen not to go to Canada, 'the American Siberia', where everything was inferior to the United States and the country was filled with Orangemen.

In the first half of the nineteenth century it was common practice for a young husband (or occasionally a wife) to emigrate alone in the hope of earning or borrowing enough to bring out their family after a year or so. A husband wrote to his Galway wife in 1848:

> I send home this 10 pound; I hope that it will not be long until I send for ye all. I would make arrangements to send for some of ye, but I expect to bring ye all from Liverpool. I would rather ye would be all together than to separate ye from each other … I hope that my fine children is all together …We are all very clean here; every one in this country wash their faces and comes [sic] their hair three times a day.

According to *The First Report from His Majesty's Commissioners for Inquiring into the Condition of the Poorer Classes in Ireland (1835)* in Longford sometimes, 'a married man, driven to despair by his hopeless condition, takes the extreme step of deserting his family, and absconding to America, leaving his wife and children with very slender means of subsistence', though always with the 'fixed intention' of sending for them when able. During the Famine, husbands were particularly inclined to exploit the public relief system; able-bodied men would desert their families and, 'proceed to America immediately, and probably they are not heard of for months, and a great many when they get out there marry again; they forget that they have wives and families at home, and their wives and families remain as permanent paupers in the workhouse.'

The vast majority of those who fled the Famine had to raise the money for their passage. America remained the most popular destination during the Famine years. If this could not be raised through the sale of their stock or their interest in the farm, there was also the possibility of help from those who had already settled in the United States. Michael Rush of Ardglass, Co Down, wrote to his parents in America requesting their help:

> Now my dear father and mother, if you knew what hunger we and our fellow-countrymen are suffering, you could take us out of this poverty Isle … If you don't endeavour to take us out of it, it will be the first news you will hear by some friend of me and my little family to be lost by the hunger, and there are thousands dread they will share the same fate.

The United States government had by this time imposed strict controls on its passenger vessels and this had helped push up fares. Lower standards on British crossings to Canada meant that fares could sometimes be as low as £3 per person – one third of the price of a passage to New York. Vessels carrying goods from St

Lawrence and Newfoundland to British ports gladly accepted destitute Irish into their holds as ballast. These were the infamous 'coffin ships', grossly overcrowded and inadequately provided with food and clean water. As a result, the Famine Fever flourished. At Grosse Isle, where a quarantine station had been established, Stephen de Vere noted in his diary that 'water covered with beds cooking vessels etc. of the dead. Ghastly appearance of boats full of sick going ashore never to return. Several died between ship and shore. Wives separated from husbands, children from parents, etc'.

After about 1850, as rural society stabilised and the removal of entire households became less common, another model of chain emigration became predominant. In 1852 an Armagh linen merchant, who had handled numerous remittances and 'thousands of their letters', discerned 'almost an organised system' in his locality: 'a son or daughter goes first, acquires some money, and sends it home … the money which is sent takes out another member of the family, and at length the whole family go'. This system enabled the surplus children of rural households to emigrate successively.

From the 1850s it was the wealth abroad, rather than destitution at home, which attracted emigration. As Jules de Lasteryrie wrote in 1860, 'it is no longer the destitution of Ireland, but the wealth of Canada, of the United States, and of Australia, which now promotes Irish emigration.' Coulter found when he travelled through the West of Ireland in the early 1860s:

> There is scarcely a family in Clare which has not some member or members in America or Australia, and remittances are constantly being sent by these exiles to their relatives at home. Sometimes the old couple receive five or six pounds from their son, whose horny hand need never lie idle in his bosom in the new world. Sometimes, as in a case which was lately mentioned to me, a young girl earning good wages in America, sends several pounds to her brother, who is willing to work, but can find no employment in his own country. The large sums thus sent home by Irish emigrants have often excited surprise and elicited the warmest admiration, as proofs of the deep-seated feelings of family affection which characterise our people.

He noted that the Civil War in America had latterly led to a noticeable decrease in such remittances. Others saw emigration as a positive sign. James McCauley wrote in 1872:

> It is sad to see everywhere the deserted villages, and ruined homesteads, and roofless cabins. But these ruined houses are in reality marks of the country's progress, as much as the ruined castles and fortresses are marks of the 'bad

old times' which have passed away. In the times when 'every rood of ground maintained its man' it was a poor and precarious maintenance at the best, and always on the verge of starvation by famine, which did come at last. The emigration, which then began to flow in earnest, saved the country.

Potential emigrants were encouraged by published accounts of America and Canada in local newspapers. The *Armagh Guardian* ran a series of articles in 1849 entitled 'Life in the Backwoods of America: Experiences in the West'. Although there was no attempt to deny the harshness of life in the backwoods, especially during the winter months, these tales were written with a Jack London sense of adventure. 'Real poverty is almost unknown', the author declared, 'the high wages, and low prices of flour, meat and potatoes, enabling every industrious man to provide for his family; and the only cases of real distress I met with were occasioned by protected illness and reckless mismanagement'. He then

Interior view of a peasant cottage. (*Illustrated London News*, 27 February 1846)

recounted a tale of how he had unintentionally offended a family who were living in a miserable shanty in the forest:

> The man came to chop for us, and showed a bite on his face and arm, which he had received from rats, by which their home was infested. 'Fact is,' he added, 'there ain't much for them to eat besides.' Moved by his plight our hero arranged that the family should have a proper English Christmas, with a turkey and a plum pudding and a local Doctor provided a bottle of sherry. The next day the man said nothing so that the narrator was forced to ask how had he enjoyed the plum pudding. 'Oh yes', the man replied, 'it was good enough; but oughtn't there to have been wine sauce? I thought that always went with plum pudding! The turkey was too fat; my woman says all the goodness went in the cooking. And that was all the thanks our hardy backwoodsman received for his generosity.

If life for the men was hard, life for female emigrants was harder still. The article in the *Armagh Guardian* conceded as much:

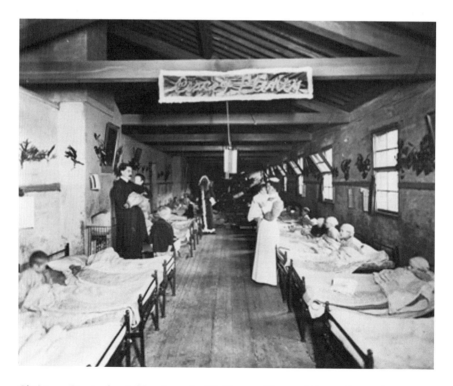

Christmas Day in the children's ward of Belfast workhouse. (Ulster Museum)

A woman's life in the West is necessarily a hard and a busy one, far more so than falls to the lot of the men, for their labour ends with the day, and in winter they have little to do, whilst their wives have abundant employment all the year round; and in harvest time, although the men work from earliest dawn until the last glimmer of light had disappeared, their wives have to work far into the night to prepare the meals for the following day.

Despite these hardships it has been estimated that women formed about half the numbers of those who emigrated during the nineteenth century. Before the Great Famine most travelled as part of a family group or childless married couples. By the late Victorian era females formed a majority of those emigrating. More than half of these were unmarried, leaving by choice, hoping for better prospects in America or the colonies. Most ended up in domestic service in America, where it was estimated that as many as 43 per cent of domestic servants were Irish. Figures also suggest that the vast majority of women who emigrated later married in their adopted country.

In order to meet the great demand for farmers and agricultural labourers, the Canadian government offered assisted passages to married agricultural labourers when accompanied by their families and to servant girls at £2 per adult, £1 for children under one year and 6s 8d for infants under 12 months. In addition, the government of Ontario offered free passes from Quebec to any part of the province of Ontario, and a grant to each person twelve years of age and over, of the sum of $6 or £1 4s 8d when three months in the Province, the provision of employment with farmers and others for any person requiring it.

From his office at 3 Patrick Street, Cork, an emigration commissioner named J. Murphy travelled about the southern counties during the 1870s delivering lectures on 'The advantages of Ontario as a suitable field for Irish emigration'. The advantages were obvious; the Province of Ontario consisted of about 20,000 square miles, larger than England, Scotland and Wales put together. The government of the province was offering every head of a family 200 acres, and for every child eighteen years and over an additional 100 acres. All the occupant needed to do was to build a log cabin 16 feet by 20 feet, clear about 2 acres to every 100 per annum and reside upon the land six months in every year. At the end of five years from the date of location, the settler received his patent from the government and he became his own landlord for ever. As J. Murphy commented, 'he must be a worthless man, indeed, if he be not able to make a comfortable living for himself and family for which he pays no rent and but a few shillings a year taxation'.

Letters written by family already in Canada also played their part in attracting emigrants. One such emigrant was Isaac Topley who wrote to his family at Markethill in County Armagh. In a letter written at the time of the Great Famine in Ireland he declared:

> the winter here is very pleasant. I can work with my coat off all day, the winter is getting something like home, the snow is not more than 2 or 3 inches deep this winter as yet, everyday is like a Christmas here for eating and drinking there is so many thing(s) on the table we do not know what to eat.

Issac's brother Abraham, writing to their brother-in-law James Boardman at Tandragee a few years later, passed on news of their sister Elizabeth. He also told them that he was thinking of getting married:

> I was thinking of looking for a woman as the people is advising me to marry. I believe I could get one … she [has] fifty acres of good land and has the deed in her own name but she has four children. She is from Comber below Belfast the people advise me not to take her on the account of her having a family, so I think I will not heed it now nor never with the same …

In 1871 the first census of the dominion of Canada was taken. The Irish were found to be 24.3 per cent of the entire population, making them the largest English-language ethnic group. In Ontario, the heartland of English-speaking Canada, persons of Irish origins were 34.5 per cent of the population, by far the largest ethnic group.

Australian emigration, as a mass organised movement, did not get going in a major way until the 1820s, after the disruption of the Napoleonic Wars. The distance involved and the logistics of the journey meant that the numbers going to Australia compared to North America were much smaller. Before the 1830s Australia attracted those who were generally better off than those who left Ireland for North America. Few Irish emigrants could afford the full fare of about £17. Australia therefore attracted a significant proportion of emigrants with the resources to set themselves up in business or on the land in the expanding agricultural hinterland of the coastal settlements. One such person was Henry Osborne who left his father's substantial County Tyrone farm in 1828 and invested the £1,000 his father gave him as a farewell gift in Irish linen which, on his arrival in Sydney, he is reputed to have sold at a fine profit. Osborne received two land grants, each of 2,560 acres at Marshall Mount. By 1854 Osborne held 261,000 acres, a large portion of which he leased from the government at less than one-fifth of a penny per acre per year, including land which contained the valuable coalfields at Newcastle.

Emigrant letters were an important source of inducement to those who had
remained at home and these were often published in local newspapers. David
Fairley and his wife from the city of Derry emigrated to Australia in 1837. His
letter from Sydney to his brother James in February 1838 was published in the
Londonderry Sentinel:

> I joined the government work with the rest of my shipmates, as a bricklayer,
> at two guineas per week, which is regularly paid every Saturday … we are
> employed in the Governor's botanic gardens … we could reach almost off
> our scaffolds to the lemons and oranges, fig trees, pomegranates, peaches etc
> and the parrots sitting on the trees beside us in flocks … all differing from
> the northern part of the globe.

By the 1830s there were a number of sponsored or assisted passages. The
following advertisement appeared in the *Londonderry Sentinel* from July to
September 1836:

> Her Majesty's government, in order to encourage the emigration of industri-
> ous young married couples to the Australian colonies, will now grant towards
> the expenses of their passage a bounty or free gift of £20 for each married
> couple without regard to their trade or occupation … thus a man and wife
> who are possessed of £18 may be conveyed free to Van Diemen's Land or
> Sydney with all provisions for the voyage …

Life in the bush.

After 1856 each of the four main colonies, New South Wales, Tasmania, Victoria and South Australia developed its own assisted scheme and some had more than one. These ranged from land guarantees to free passages. Recent studies have suggested than 64 per cent of all immigrants up to 1850, 34 per cent in the gold rush era and 51 per cent from 1860-1900 were assisted. The Irish were quick to understand the mechanism of assisted migration so that although they were only about 30 per cent of the total population of the British Isles, they made up 52 per cent of the assisted migrants to New South Wales and to the Port Phillip District (later Victoria) in the period 1837-50.

An earlier source of free passages at the expense of the authorities was con- vict transportation. Some of those transported went on to carve a new and prosperous life for themselves. One such emancipated convict Robert Boyde, writing from Modbury County, Murray, New South Wales, told his family that 'I am happy to inform you that I am master of sixteen head of cattle which I have bought at different times with money earned after doing my government work'. James Halloran, an Irish convict in Australia, echoed these views in a letter he wrote to his wife in 1840:

> We sailed on the 6th of July and landed on the 29th of January eighteen hun- dred and forty and D[ea]r Catherine if you can in the world get one pound for yourself and the child, and come to the immigrant office in Dublin and come to this country and if you can bring my brother John with you and he will get out for the same, this is the best country under the sun, for any well behaved person labourer man will get from thirty to forty pounds pr year … I am very thankful to my prosecutors for sending me here to the land of liberty and freedom.

The voyage to Australia was long and arduous. Even those who paid their way could be subjected to something approaching naval discipline during the long voyage. James Dempsey, sailing from Derry in 1838, discovered that 'if anyone is found pilfering … or giving insolence … or refusing to clean their berths or sweep upper and lower decks … when they arrived at Sidney, will be given up to the government and punished in proportion.' For those of a more refined nature, the amusements on board ship were almost as bad as the brutal discipline. Elizabeth Anketell, from Aughnacloy in County Tyrone, was far from amused at the initiation ceremony aimed at those who were 'crossing the line' for the first time. A passenger on the *Queen of Australia*, she complained:

I cannot enjoy these nasty jokes – the victim is placed on a stool, held by two men blackened all over to represent Negroes; Neptune and his wife dressed up in the most hideous manner, sit in front. A large brush, dipped in pitch and tar is put all over the face and into the mouth if possible … he is rolled down into a tank of sea water and nearly smothered by the two Negroes … I had to pay a fine of three shillings and kiss Mrs Neptune – this I certainly did not calculate on.

It offended her very Victorian sense of propriety that when she had put some clothing out to dry, members of the crew hoisted them 'to the highest mast on the ship'. William Bates, a young Presbyterian clergyman from Strabane in County Tyrone, was equally upset by what he saw as the sudden desertion of spiritual virtues on board ship. He complained that, 'Our young men seem indifferent to religion … they crowned the Sabbath evening's impropriety by closing Mr Bowman [a fellow cleric] in the water closet, tying the doors together with a rope.'

With this mass exodus of the Great Famine, emigration was to become an important factor in Irish society during the next one hundred years. Many travellers to Ireland commented on it. Dr David Forbes, who travelled around Ireland during the autumn of 1852, arrived at Killaloe, twelve miles from Limerick, to join the steamer for a pleasure cruise to Athlone where he came across a party of emigrants. They were all making their way to Liverpool via Dublin. The majority of them were going to the United States, but several, particularly the young women, were bound for Australia. Dr Forbes was moved by the distressful scenes he witnessed at the quayside:

With the utter unconsciousness and disregard of being observed of all observers, which characterises authentic sorrow, these warm-hearted and simple-minded people demeaned themselves entirely as if they had been shrouded in all the privacy of home, clinging to and kissing and embracing each other with the utmost ardour, calling out aloud, in broken tones, the endeared names of brother, sister, mother, sobbing and crying as if the very heart would burst, while the unheeded tears ran down from the red and swollen eyes literally in streams.

More than 8 million people left Ireland between 1801 and 1921, making it one of the greatest mass migrations in world history; approximately 1 million people left the country between 1846 and 1850 alone. Those who remained and who survived the Great Famine had to deal with massive social changes brought about by the blight. The ramshackle economy, which had grown up during the Napoleonic Wars, had been destroyed and the persistent problem of unemployment had been eradicated. Uniquely in Europe, Ireland's population shrank from 8 million in 1841 to 4 million eighty years later. Whether it was serving as an administrator in Canada or panning for gold in Australia, the impact of Irish emigration has been out of proportion to Ireland's status as a small country on the outskirts of Europe. Its chief legacy is that today no less than 70 million people around the world can claim Irish descent.

★ Postscript ★

Queen Victoria visited Ireland for the last time between 4 and 25 April 1900; she wished to acknowledge the exceptional heroism of her Irish soldiers during the war in South Africa. The Royal Yacht arrived at Kingstown to the thunder of heavy guns and the cheering multitude which had been making its way to the decorated barriers which surrounded the wharf. As the Queen made her way to the waiting carriage, the combined bands of the *Majestic* and *Magnificent* played the national anthem and the waiting crowds waved thousands of miniature Union Jacks.

The Queen made her public entry into Dublin to the cheers of enthusiastic crowds on a typical spring day. The *Irish Times* reported that:

> The band stationed at the junction of Grafton and Nassau streets played the National Anthem, but the strains of the music were drowned in the thunder of the cheers of a great multitude. As Her Majesty's carriage passed through College Green the National Anthem was sung by the occupants of the various stands, innumerable flags were waved, and the din of cheering was deafening. The effect was unrehearsed. It could by no means have been provided for. But in the result it was magnificent. The Queen's reception was worthy of Dublin and of the occasion, and, if it be not presumptuous to say so, Her Majesty must have been surprised at it. All Ireland is now her bodyguard. All Irishmen are her loyal lieges. We may differ in politics, and we shall do so to the end of the chapter, but there is not one Irish gentleman or gentlewoman who ever will swerve in allegiance to the Queen.

Those who witnessed these events could not have imagined a more fitting conclusion to a century which had seen Ireland take its rightful place in the Empire; agrarian violence was in decline, Home Rule appeared dead and successive British governments had transferred the land from the once all-

Four Courts, Dublin. (W.H. Bartlett, *The Scenery and Antiquities of Ireland*, 1841)

powerful landlords to their tenants. Throughout the Empire the Irish were a conspicuous presence as soldiers, administrators, clergy and settlers. At the beginning of the twentieth century it seemed as if Ireland at peace would remain forever at the heart of the British Empire. To the shivering crowds of April 1900, war, rebellion and partition were the concerns of other, less civilised, parts of the globe.

BIBLIOGRAPHY

Contemporary Sources

Ashworth, John Hervey, *The Saxon in Ireland*, 1851.

Atkinson, A., *Ireland in the 19th c. & Seventh of England's Dominion*, 1844.

Austin, Alfred, *Spring & Autumn in Ireland*, 1900.

Bayne, Samuel Gamble, *On an Irish Jaunting-car through Donegal & Connemara*, 1902.

Binns, Jonathan, *Miseries and Beauties of Ireland*, 1837.

Burke, Oliver Joseph, *The South Isles of Aran (County Galway)*, 1887.

Caldwell, J.M., *Old Irish Life*, 1912.

Cobbett, William, ed. G.D.H. & Margaret Col *Rural rides*.

Cooke, Thomas L., *Autumnal Rambles about New Quay, County Clare* (from: *Galway Vindicator*), 1842-3.

Coulter, Henry, *The West of Ireland: its existing conditions and prospects*, 1862.

Croker, Thomas Crofton, *Researches in the South of Ireland*, 1824.

Curwen, John Christian, *Observations on the state of Ireland*.

de Bovet, Madame, *Three Month's Tour in Ireland*, 1891.

de Tocqueville, Alexis, *Journey in Ireland*, 1835.

East, John, *Glimpses of Ireland in 1847*, 1847.

Elizabeth, Charlotte, *Letters from Ireland*, 1837/1838.

Forbes, John, *Memorandums made in Ireland in the autumn of 1852*, 1853.

Foster, Thomas Campbell, *Letters on the condition of the people of Ireland*, 1846.

Gamble, John, *A View of Society and Manners in the North of Ireland in the Summer and Autumn of 1812*, 1813.

Grousset, Paschal, *Ireland's Disease: notes and impressions*, 1888.

Gwynn, Stephen Lucius, *Highways & Byways in Donegal & Antrim*, 1899.

H.B.H., *Holiday Haunts on the West Coast of Clare*, 1891.

Haight, Canniff, *Here & there in the Home Land: England, Scotland & Ireland, as seen by a Canadian*, 1895.

Hall, James, *Tour Through Ireland*, 1813.

Hall, Samuel Carter, *Ireland, Its Scenery, Character & History*, 1846.

Hurlbert, William Henry, *Ireland Under Coercion: The Diary of an American*, 1888.

Inglis, Henry D., *A Journey Through Ireland*, 1834.

Johnson, Clifton, *The Isle of the Shamrock*, 1901.

Johnson, James, *A Tour of Ireland with Meditations and Reflections*, 1844.

Johnston, Charles, *Ireland, Historic & Picturesque, c.* 1901.

Lovett, Richard, *Ireland Illustrated with Pen and Pencil, c.* 1891.

Lynd, Robert, *Rambles in Ireland*, 1912.

M'Manus, Henry, *Sketches of the Irish Highlands: Description, Social & Religious, w/special ref. to Irish missions in West Con*, 1863

Macaulay, James, *Ireland in 1872; a tour of observation.*

McDougall, Margaret Dixon, *The Letters of 'Norah' on her Tour Through Ireland*, 1882.

Nicholson, Asenath, (Hatch) *The Bible in Ireland; Ireland's welcome to the stranger, or Excursions through Ireland in 1844-5*, 1847

Osborne, Sidney Godolphin, *Gleanings from the West of Ireland*, 1850.

Otway, Caesar, *A tour in Connaught: comprising sketches of Clonmacnoise, Joyce*, 1839.

Sullivan, A.M., *New Ireland*, 1877.

Russell, Thomas O'Neill, *Beauties & Antiquities of Ireland: A Tourist's Guide to its most Beautiful Scenery and an Archaeologist's Manual*, 1897.

Thackeray, William Makepeace, *The Irish Sketch Book,* 1887.

Walker, William Wesley, *An Itinerant in the British Isles*, 1896.

Statistical Surveys of the Royal Dublin Society

J. Dubourdieu, *Antrim*, 1812.

Sir Charles Coote, *Armagh*, 1802.

Sir Charles Coote, *Cavan*, 1802.

Hely Dutton, *Clare*, 1808.

Horatio Townsend, *Cork*, 2 volumes, 1815.

J. Dubourdieu, *Down*, 1802.

Joseph Archer, *Dublin*, 1801.

Hely Dutton, *Galway*, 1824.

Thomas James Rawson, *Kildare*, 1807.

William Tighe, *Kilkenny*, 1802.

Sir Charles Coote, *King's County*, 1801.

James McParlan, *Leitrim*, 1802.

Revd George V. Sampson, *Londonderry*, 1802.

Robert Thompson, *Meath*, 1802.

Sir Charles Coote, *Monaghan*, 1801.

Sir Charles Coote, *Queen's County*, 1801.

Isaac Weld, *Roscommon*, 1832.

James McParlan, *Sligo*, 1802.

John McEvoy, *Tyrone*, 1802.

Robert Fraser, *Wexford*, 1807.

Robert Fraser, *Wicklow*, 1801.

Selected Secondary Sources

Akenson, Donald Harman, *The Irish Diaspora: A Primer* (Belfast, 1995).

Bardon, Jonathan, *A History of Ulster* (Belfast, 1992).

Bartlett, Tom and Jeffrey, Keith (eds), *A Military History of Ireland* (Cambridge, 1996).

Beckett, J.C., *The Making of Modern Ireland, 1603-1923* (London, 1966).

J.C. Beckett & R.E. Glasscock (eds.), *Belfast: The Origin and Growth of an Industrial City* (London, 1967).

Bourke, Angela, *The Burning of Bridget Cleary* (London, 1999).

Bew, Paul, *Land and the National Question in Ireland, 1858-82* (Humanities Press, 1979).

Bourke, Joanna, *From Husbandry to Housewifery: Women, Economic Change and Housework in Ireland 1890-1914* (Oxford, 1993).

Boyce, D. George, *Nineteenth-century Ireland: The Search for Stability* (Dublin, 1990).

Boyce, D. George, *Nationalism in Ireland* (Routledge, 1996).

Brown, Terence, *Ireland: A Social and Cultural History* (New York, 1985).

Brynn, Edward, *Crown & Castle: British Rule in Ireland, 1800-1830* (Dublin, 1978).

Collins, B., (1993), 'The Irish in Britain, 1780-1921' in B.J. Graham and L.J. Connolly, S.J. (ed) *The Oxford Companion To Irish History* (Oxford, 1998).

Coogan, Tim Pat, *Wherever Green is Worn: the story of the Irish Diaspora* (London, 2000).

Connell, K.H., *The Population of Ireland, 1750-1845* (Clarendon Press, 1950).

Connolly, S., (1987), *Religion and Society in Nineteenth Century Ireland*, Dundalk.

Crawford, W.H., & Trainor, B. *Aspects of Irish Social History, 1750–1800* (Belfast 1969).

Cronin, Denis A., Jim Gilligan, & Karina Holton (eds.), *Irish Fairs and Markets* (Four Courts Press, 2001).

Crossman, Virginia, *Politics, Pauperism and Power in Nineteenth-Century Ireland* (Manchester, 2006).

Crossman, Virginia, *The Poor Law in Ireland, 1838-1948.* (Dundalk, 2006).

Cullen, L.M. (ed.), *Six Generations: Life and Work in Ireland from 1750* (Mercier Press, 1970).

Cunningham, Terence P., *The Church since Emancipation: Church Reorganization* (Gill & Macmillan, 1970).

Curtis, Jr, L. Perry, *Apes and Angles: The Irishman in Victorian Caricature* (Smithsonian Institution Press, 1997).

Daly, Mary E., *Social and Economic History of Ireland since 1800* (Educational Company of Ireland, 1981).

de Nie, Michael, *The Eternal Paddy: Irish Identity and the British Press, 1798-1882* (University of Wisconsin Press, 2004).

Evans, E.E., *Irish Folk Ways* (Routledge and Kegan Paul, 1957).

Fitzpatrick, D., *Irish Emigration 1801-1921* (Dundalk, 1985).

Fitzpatrick, D., *Oceans of Consolation: Personal Accounts of Irish Emigration to Australia* (Cork, 1995).

Foster, R.F. *Charles Stewart Parnell: The Man and His Family* (Harvester, 1979).

Green, E.R.R. (ed) *Essays in Scotch-Irish History* (Belfast, 1969).

Hachey, Thomas E., *Britain and Irish Separatism: From the Fenians to the Free State, 1867-1922* (Rand McNally, 1977).

Hempton, C. & Hill, M. *Evangelical Protestantism in Ulster Society 1740-1890* (London, 1992).

Hoppen, K.T., *Ireland Since 1800: Conflict and Conformity* (London, 1989).

Horgan, Donal, *The Victorian Visitor in Ireland: Irish Tourism 1840-1910* (Imagimedia, 2002).

Jackson, A., *The Ulster Party: Irish Unionists in the House of Commons 1886-1911* (Oxford, 1989).

Jackson, A., *Home Rule: An Irish History 1800-2000* (London, 2003).

Kearns, Kevin C., *Dublin Tenement Life: An Oral History* (Penguin, 1994).

Keenan, D., *The Catholic Church in Nineteenth-Century Ireland: A Sociological Study* (Dublin, 1983).

Kinealy, C., *The Great Calamity: The Irish Famine 1845-52* (Dublin, 1994).

Larkin, Emmet J., *The Roman Catholic Church and the Home Rule Movement in Ireland, 1870-1874* (University of North Carolina Press, 2009).

Larkin, Emmet J., *The Roman Catholic Church in Ireland and the Fall of Parnell, 1888-1891* (University of North Carolina Press, 1979).

Lyons, F.S.L., *Ireland since the Famine* (Charles Scribner's Sons, 1971).

MacRaild, Donald M., *The Irish Diaspora in Britain, 1750-1939 (Social History in Perspective),* (London, 2010).

Maxwell, I., *Researching Irish Ancestors* (Barnsley, 2008).

Murphy, James H. (ed.), *Evangelicals and Catholics in Nineteenth-Century Ireland* (Four Courts Press, 2005).

Ó Gráda, C., *Ireland: A New Economic History 1780-1939* (Oxford, 1994).

Ó Gráda, C. *Ireland Before and After the Famine* (Manchester, 1988).

Ó Gráda, C., *The Great Irish Famine* (London, 1989).

O'Shea, J., *Priests, Politics and Society in Post-Famine Ireland* (Dublin, 1983).

O'Tuathaigh, M. A. G., 'The Irish in nineteenth-century Britain. Problems of integration', *Transactions of the Royal Historical Society*, 21 (1981).

Scally, Robert James, *The End of Hidden Ireland: Rebellion, Famine, and Emigration* (Oxford University Press, 1995).

Townshend, Charles, *Political Violence in Ireland* (Oxford University Press, 1985).

Whelan, B. (ed), *Women and Work in Ireland* (Dublin, 2000), pp. 51-62.

Vaughan, W. E., *Landlords and Tenants in Victorian Ireland* (Oxford, 1994).

If you enjoyed this book, you may also be interested in...

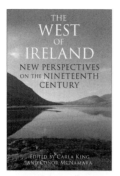

The West of Ireland:
New Perspectives on the Nineteenth Century

EDITED BY CARLA KING AND CONOR MCNAMARA

The West of Ireland: New Perspectives on the Nineteenth Century examines the struggles of ordinary people in the west of Ireland throughout a century characterised by unprecedented social and economic upheaval. Featuring contributions from some of Ireland's most established academics, along with a number of younger historians, this study shines a light on lesser-known aspects of the evolution of a complex rural society undergoing a traumatic process of economic modernisation.

978 1 84588 705 6

1916 and All That:
A History of Ireland From Back Then Until Right Now

C.M. BOYLAN

C.M. Boylan's wonderfully irreverent take on the history of Ireland will take you from the 'Age of the Third Best Metal', through the struggles of Wolfe Tone (Ireland's best-named revolutionary), right through the Celtic Tiger years, when there was pancetta and rubies for all. And then on to the present day, when there are fewer rubies. And, on the way, this book is not afraid to ask the hard questions, such as: Why were walls so important for the Normans? And can you describe and explain Limerick?

978 1 84588 749 0

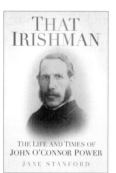

That Irishman:
The Life and Times of John O'Connor Power

JANE STANFORD

The story of John O'Connor Power is the story of Ireland's struggle for nationhood itself. Born into poverty in Ballinasloe in 1846 he eventually became a powerful political force. He was one of a distinguished company, that indomitable Irishry of Charles Stewart Parnell, Michael Davitt and Isaac Butt, who made the dream of an independent Ireland a reality.

978 1 84588 698 1

Jewish Ireland: A Social History

RAY RIVLIN

Jewish Ireland: A Social History is an engaging and thoroughly researched panorama of Irish Jewry. Based on library and archival material, private memoirs and oral testimony, it traces Irish-Jewish life from the 1880s when Orthodox Russian Jews, forced to flee Tsarist persecution, began arriving in Ireland, to the present day.

978 1 84588 708 7

Visit our website and discover thousands of other History Press books.

www.thehistorypress.ie